Illustrated Study Bible

Illustrated Study Bible

Selection from material compiled by

Frank H. Meade and Arnold W. Zimmermann

Illustrated by Shirley Smith and H. H. Turner
First published by Holmes McDougall Limited, Edinburgh, Scotland

JUDSON PRESS
Valley Forge

ILLUSTRATED STUDY BIBLE

Library of Congress Cataloging in Publication Data

Bible. English. Authorized. Selections. 1973.
    Illustrated study Bible.

    SUMMARY: Old and New Testament Bible selections accompanied by illustrations and brief text portraying the way of life in Biblical times and countries.
    [1. Bible—Selections. 2. Bible—Antiquities] I. Meade, F. H. M. II. Zimmermann, Arnold Walter. III. Smith, Shirley, illus. IV. Turner, H. H., illus. V. Bible. English. Selections. 1960. Authorized. The school study Bible. VI. Title.
BS391.2.M4   220.5'203   72-9567
ISBN 0-8170-0583-8

Printed in the U.S.A.

Contents

                                                                              Page
A Word to the Reader   9

THE OLD TESTAMENT
Stories of the Early Hebrews
    Abram—His Call and Journey   Genesis 12:1-10   10
    Jacob and Esau   Genesis 25:20-34; 27:1-45   12
    Jacob's Reunion with Esau   Genesis 32:3-8; 33   14
    Joseph and His Brethren   Genesis 37   14
    Joseph in Egypt   Genesis 39:1-6, 21-23   18
    Joseph in Prison   Genesis 40   18
    Joseph Is Made Ruler   Genesis 41   20
    The Coming of His Brethren   Genesis 42-45   24
    The Coming of the Israelites to Egypt   Genesis 46:2-6, 28-34;
                                                                       48:1-12; 49:1, 33   26

Moses—the Hero of Faith
    Moses' Childhood—Flight from Egypt   Exodus 1, 2   28
    The Burning Bush   Exodus 3   30
    Moses Is Given Proof   Exodus 4   30
    In Egypt   Exodus 7:1-13   32
    Going Out of Egypt   Exodus 12:1-11; 13:17-22;
                                                                       14; 15:20-27   34
    In the Wilderness   Exodus 16, 18   36
    Mount Sinai   Exodus 24:12-18; 20:1-18   39
    The Promised Land   Deuteronomy 8:1-14   42
Deborah—Heroine and Liberator   Judges 4   44
Ruth and Naomi   Ruth 1; 2; 4:13-17   46
Samuel
    The Birth of Samuel, Early Days in the Temple   1 Samuel 1:9-28; 2:12-35   48
    The Lord's Voice   1 Samuel 3:1-20   51
Saul Is Chosen   1 Samuel 9, 10   53
Saul and David
    David's Anointment   1 Samuel 16   56
    Jonathan and Saul's Jealousy   1 Samuel 18:1-16; 19:1-12   60
    David's Escape from Saul   1 Samuel 20   60
    Sparing Saul's Life   1 Samuel 24   64
    Death of Saul   1 Samuel 31   66
    News Brought to David   2 Samuel 1   66
David the King
    His Kindness   2 Samuel 4:4; 9   68
    "Thou Art the Man"   2 Samuel 11:1-3, 14-17,
                                                                    26-27; 12:1-10, 13-24   69
    Absalom   2 Samuel 15:1-6, 10-14; 18 72
Solomon
    Chosen to Be King   1 Kings 1:1, 28-40; 2:1-4, 10   74

Building the Temple	1 Kings 5; 6:7	76
Elijah		
Fed by the Ravens	1 Kings 17:1-7	79
The Widow's Cruse	1 Kings 17:8-15	80
Healing the Woman's Son	1 Kings 17:17-24	80
The Prophets of Baal	1 Kings 18:1-40	82
Under the Juniper Tree	1 Kings 19:1-8	86
The Still Small Voice	1 Kings 19:9-18	87
The Mantle of Elijah	1 Kings 19:19-21	88
(Isaiah—Hezekiah) Sennacherib	Isaiah 36, 37	90
Jerusalem Taken	2 Kings 25:1-4, 8-10	93
The Captivity	Jeremiah 29:1-14	93
Daniel—The Golden Image	Daniel 3:1-19	94
Return to Jerusalem		
Rebuilding the Temple	Ezra 1, 3, 6; Haggai 1	98
Rebuilding the Walls of the City	Nehemiah 1, 2, 4, 6	100

THE NEW TESTAMENT

The Birth and Childhood of Jesus		
At Bethlehem	Luke 2:1-7	102
The Shepherds	Luke 2:8-20	104
The Wise Men	Matthew 2:1-12	106
The Flight to Egypt	Matthew 2:13-23; Luke 2:40	108
Jesus in the Temple	Luke 2:41-52	110
The Preparation for His Ministry		
The Preaching of John the Baptist	Matthew 3:1-12	112
The Baptism of Jesus	Mark 1:9-11	112
The Ministry of Jesus		
The First Disciples	Mark 1:16-20	114
Simon's Mother-in-law	Mark 1:29-31	114
The Paralytic	Mark 2:1-12	116
The Call to Matthew	Matthew 9:9-13	118
The Birds and the Flowers	Matthew 6:25-34	120
The House Built on a Rock	Matthew 7:24-27	120
The Sower	Mark 4:3-20	122
The Weeds in the Corn	Matthew 13:24-30	124
The Mustard Seed	Matthew 13:31-32	124
The Mission	Mark 6:7-13	126
Walking on the Water	Matthew 14:22-36	126
The Good Samaritan	Luke 10:25-37	128
Martha and Mary	Luke 10:38-42	130
The Pharisee and the Publican	Luke 18:9-14	130
Invitation to a Feast	Luke 14:7-14	132
Parable of the Great Supper	Luke 14:16-24	132
Parable of the Lost Sheep	Luke 15:3-7	134
Parable of the Lost Silver	Luke 15:8-10	134
Parable of the Prodigal Son	Luke 15:11-32	136

The Death of Jesus
    The Triumphal Entry   Mark 11:1-11   138

The Death of Jesus		
The Triumphal Entry	Mark 11:1-11	138
The Cleansing of the Temple	Mark 11:15-19	140
The Widow's Mite	Mark 12:41-44	140
The Talents	Matthew 25:14-30	142
The Foolish Virgins	Matthew 25:1-13	144
The Conspiracy	Mark 14:1-11	146
The Last Supper	Mark 14:12-31	148
Washing the Disciples' Feet	John 13:1-17	150
Peter's Protest	Luke 22:31-34	150
The Arrest	Mark 14:32-52	152
Peter's Denial	Luke 22:54-62	154
Trial Before Pilate	Mark 15:1-15	156
The Crucifixion	Mark 15:16-39	158
The Embalmment and Burial of Jesus	Mark 15:40-47	160
The Resurrection of Jesus		
The Empty Tomb	Mark 16:1-8	162
Jesus and Mary Magdalene	John 20:11-18	164
Emmaus	Luke 24:13-35	166
Thomas, the Doubter	John 20:24-29	168
Jesus by the Sea of Galilee	John 21:1-23	168
The Ascension	Mark 16:19-20	169
The Acts of the Apostles		
Pentecost	Acts 2	171
The First Miracle	Acts 3	173
Peter's Imprisonment and Escape	Acts 12:1-17	176
The Martyrdom of Stephen	Acts 7	178
Paul		
The Road to Damascus	Acts 9:1-8	180
Jupiter and Mercury	Acts 14:6-20	182
A Warning	Acts 21:8-14	182
The Arrest	Acts 21:27-40	184
Appeal to Caesar	Acts 25:1-12	186
The Shipwreck	Acts 27	186
Malta and the Road to Rome	Acts 28:1-15	190

A Word to the Reader

The Bible stories which have been included in this book tell about some of the outstanding people of the Bible. In a small book like this, many important people and events could not be included, but the reader can turn to his own copy of the Bible to read the portions that are not found here. The drawings which accompany the stories in this book will help the reader visualize other events described in the Bible which take place in similar settings.

The material in this book is in the chronological order that is generally accepted by students of the Bible. The Table of Contents shows at a glance the Bible passages that have been selected. Because the story of Jesus is taken from the Four Gospels, the Bible passages in that section are not in the order in which they would be found in the Bible.

As far as possible, the text used is the King James Version. In some places, brief summaries of the biblical narrative have been given, and square brackets are used to denote these. An asterisk at the head of a passage indicates that certain omissions have been made from the text of the Bible passage which is used.

The Old Testament

ABRAM—
HIS CALL AND JOURNEY

Now the Lord had said unto Abram, Get thee out of thy country, and from thy kindred, and from thy father's house, unto a land that I will shew thee: And I will make of thee a great nation, and I will bless thee, and make thy name great; and thou shalt be a blessing: And I will bless them that bless thee, and curse him that curseth thee: and in thee shall all families of the earth be blessed.

So Abram departed, as the Lord had spoken unto him; and Lot went with him: and Abram was seventy and five years old when he departed out of Haran. And Abram took Sarai his wife, and Lot his brother's son, and all their substance that they had gathered, and the souls that they had gotten in Haran; and they went forth to go into the land of Canaan; and into the land of Canaan they came.

And Abram passed through the land unto the place of Sichem, unto the plain of Moreh. And the Canaanite was then in the land.

And the Lord appeared unto Abram, and said, Unto thy seed will I give this land: and there builded he an altar unto the Lord, who appeared unto him. And he removed from thence unto a mountain on the east of Beth-el: and there he builded an altar unto the Lord, and called upon the name of the Lord.

And Abram journeyed, going on still toward the south.

Genesis xii.1-10

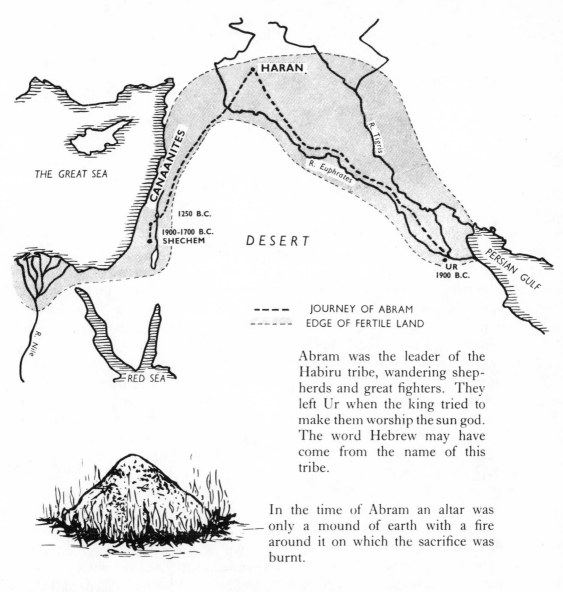

HARAN

THE GREAT SEA

CANAANITES

R. Tigris

R. Euphrates

1250 B.C.

1900-1700 B.C.
SHECHEM

DESERT

UR
1900 B.C.

PERSIAN GULF

R. Nile

RED SEA

- - - - JOURNEY OF ABRAM
- - - - - EDGE OF FERTILE LAND

Abram was the leader of the Habiru tribe, wandering shepherds and great fighters. They left Ur when the king tried to make them worship the sun god. The word Hebrew may have come from the name of this tribe.

In the time of Abram an altar was only a mound of earth with a fire around it on which the sacrifice was burnt.

A Semitic family at the time of Abram.

(From a drawing in the tomb of Khnumhotep II)

11

JACOB AND ESAU

[Twin sons were born to Isaac and Rebekah.]

And the boys grew: and Esau was a cunning hunter, a man of the field; and Jacob was a plain man, dwelling in tents. And Isaac loved Esau, because he did eat of his venison: but Rebekah loved Jacob. And Jacob sod pottage: and Esau came from the field, and he was faint. And Esau said to Jacob, Feed me, I pray thee, with that same red pottage; for I am faint. And Jacob said, Sell me this day thy birthright. And Esau said, Behold, I am at the point to die: and what profit shall this birthright do to me?

Then Jacob gave Esau bread and pottage of lentiles; and he did eat and drink, and rose up, and went his way: thus Esau despised his birthright.

*   *   *   *   *

[When Isaac was very old, and felt that he was about to die, he asked Esau to hunt some venison so that he could have a meal and then give Esau his blessing. When Rebekah heard this, she sent for her favourite son Jacob. She ordered him to get two young kids, so that she could prepare a meal, and told him that he was to take it to his father and pretend that he was Esau. Jacob, at first, had doubts whether the scheme would work: but, after being dressed in Esau's clothes, and after putting the skins of the kids over his hands and neck, so that his father would think it was Esau, who was a hairy man, he took the meal in.

Isaac was deceived because he was nearly blind, and he gave Jacob the blessing intended for Esau. When Esau returned, he begged that he too might be given a blessing. Isaac explained that he could not take away the blessing he had given to Jacob, and instead he gave Esau a different blessing.

Esau hated Jacob because of his trickery, and swore to kill him. When Rebekah heard this, she told Jacob to go to her brother Laban's house at Haran, and to stay there until Esau's temper had cooled.]

Genesis xxv.20-34; xxvii.1-45

The tent was made of animal skins sewn together with sinews. The people lived in tents because they had to move on when their animals had eaten all the grass in one place. Women had to look after the tents.

Jacob, because he was always near the tents, became his mother's favourite son.

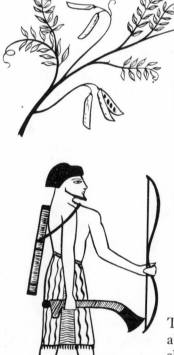

Lentils are of the pea family. The plant was cut and threshed like corn, then stewed like beans, and made into pottage. The red lentil which Jacob had cooked was a favourite dish. "Jacob sod pottage" means "Jacob boiled lentils into a dish like pease pudding."

This is the type of pot that was used for cooking over a fire of brushwood or dried dung.

This picture, drawn about 1900 B.C., shows the kind of weapons Esau may have used.

THE FIRSTBORN SON

The firstborn son was a favoured child, because he made certain that the family name would be carried on, and that wealth and leadership would stay within the male side of the family.

The same attitude can be seen today in titled families and royalty.

*JACOB'S REUNION WITH ESAU

And Jacob sent messengers before him to Esau his brother. And he commanded them, saying, Thus shall ye speak unto my lord Esau; Thy servant Jacob saith thus, I have sojourned with Laban, and stayed there until now: And I have oxen, and asses, flocks, and menservants, and womenservants: and I have sent to tell my lord, that I may find grace in thy sight.

And the messengers returned to Jacob, saying, We came to thy brother Esau, and also he cometh to meet thee, and four hundred men with him.

Then Jacob was greatly afraid: and he divided the people that was with him, and the flocks, and herds, and the camels, into two bands; and said, If Esau come to the one company, and smite it, then the other company which is left shall escape.

And Jacob lifted up his eyes, and looked, and, behold, Esau came, and with him four hundred men. And Esau ran to meet him, and embraced him, and fell on his neck, and kissed him: and they wept. And he said, What meanest thou by all this drove which I met? And Jacob said, These are to find grace in the sight of my lord. And Esau said, I have enough, my brother; keep that thou hast unto thyself. And Jacob said, Nay, I pray thee, if now I have found grace in thy sight, then receive my present at my hand. And he urged him, and he took it.

And he said, Let us take our journey, and let us go, and I will go before thee.

And Jacob said, My lord knoweth that the children are tender, and the flocks and herds with young are with me: and if men should overdrive them one day, all the flock will die. Let my lord, I pray thee, pass over before his servant: and I will lead on softly, until I come unto my lord unto Seir.

So Esau returned that day on his way unto Seir.

Genesis xxxii.3-8; xxxiii

*JOSEPH AND HIS BRETHREN

And Jacob dwelt in the land of Canaan.

Jacob loved Joseph more than all his children, because he was the son of his old age: and he made him a coat of many colours. And when his brethren saw that their father loved him more than all his brethren, they hated him, and could not speak peaceably unto him.

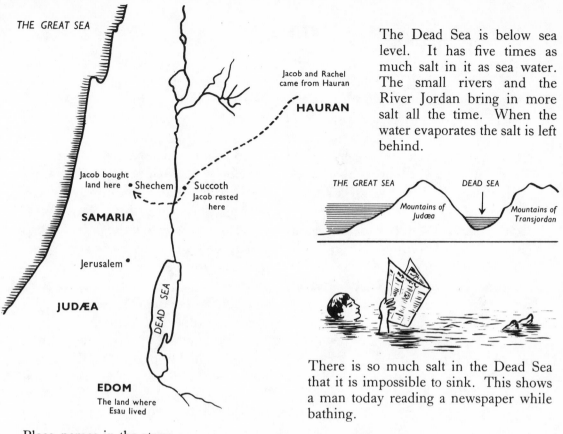

THE GREAT SEA

Jacob and Rachel
came from Hauran

HAURAN

Jacob bought
land here • Shechem • Succoth
Jacob rested
here

SAMARIA

Jerusalem •

DEAD SEA

JUDÆA

EDOM
The land where
Esau lived

Place-names in the story.

The Dead Sea is below sea level. It has five times as much salt in it as sea water. The small rivers and the River Jordan bring in more salt all the time. When the water evaporates the salt is left behind.

THE GREAT SEA   DEAD SEA

Mountains of
Judæa   Mountains of
                         Transjordan

There is so much salt in the Dead Sea that it is impossible to sink. This shows a man today reading a newspaper while bathing.

Jacob was a rich man. Riches were measured by flocks, servants, beasts of burden, and wives. Today, in Africa, many tribes still count wealth in the same way because to them money has no value.

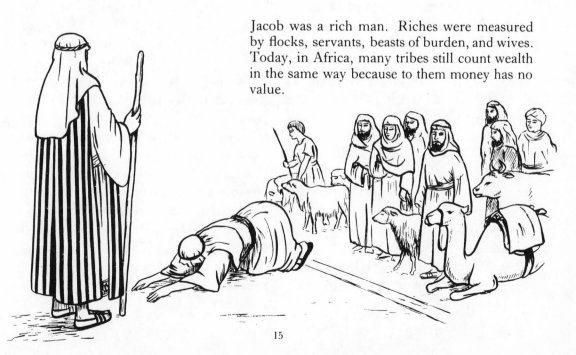

JOSEPH AND HIS BRETHREN (*Contd.*)

And Joseph dreamed a dream, and he told it his brethren: Behold, we were binding sheaves in the field, and my sheaf rose and stood upright: and your sheaves stood round about, and made obeisance to my sheaf. And his brethren said to him, Shalt thou indeed reign over us? And they hated him the more. And he dreamed yet another dream, and told it to his father and his brethren: Behold, the sun and the moon and the eleven stars made obeisance to me. And his father rebuked him, and said unto him, Shall I and thy mother and thy brethren indeed come to bow down ourselves to thee to the earth?

And his brethren went to feed their father's flock in Shechem. And Jacob said unto Joseph, Go, I pray thee, see whether it be well with thy brethren, and well with the flocks; and bring me word again.

And Joseph went after his brethren, and found them in Dothan.

And when they saw him afar off, they said one to another, Behold, this dreamer cometh. Let us slay him, and cast him into some pit, and we will say, Some evil beast hath devoured him. And Reuben heard it, and said, Let us not kill him, but cast him into this pit that is in the wilderness, that he might deliver him to his father again.

And it came to pass, when Joseph was come unto his brethren, that they stript Joseph out of his coat of many colours that was on him; and they took him, and cast him into a pit: and the pit was empty, there was no water in it.

And they sat down to eat bread: and, behold, a company of Ishmeelites came from Gilead with their camels bearing spicery and balm and myrrh, going to carry it down to Egypt. And Judah said unto his brethren, What profit is it if we slay our brother, and conceal his blood? Come, and let us sell him to the Ishmeelites. And his brethren were content.

And they lifted up Joseph out of the pit, and sold Joseph to the Ishmeelites for twenty pieces of silver. And Reuben returned unto the pit; and, behold, Joseph was not in the pit; and he rent his clothes.

And they took Joseph's coat, and killed a kid of the goats, and dipped the coat in the blood; and they brought it to their father; and said, This have we found: know now whether it be thy son's coat or no. And he knew it, and said, It is my son's coat; an evil beast hath devoured him; Joseph is without doubt rent in pieces. And Jacob rent his clothes, and put sackcloth upon his loins, and mourned for his son many days.

And the Midianites brought Joseph into Egypt and sold him unto Potiphar, an officer of Pharaoh's, and captain of the guard.

Genesis xxxvii

A Workman   A Rich Man

A workman wore a sleeveless tunic reaching to his knees.

The coat of many colours was really a tunic reaching to the feet. It was a sign of high rank. This was why Joseph's brothers became jealous.

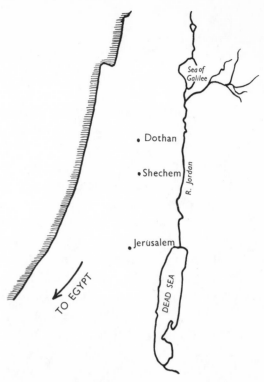

Dothan is fifteen miles north of Shechem. It means "Two cisterns".

When a Jew rent his clothes they were torn from the front of the neck to the girdle. This was a sign of mourning. Today a Jew in mourning often makes a small slit about four inches long on the right side.

A cistern was a natural water hole which had been dug more deeply and made wide at the bottom and narrow at the top. The clay lining held in the water. Cisterns filled up in the rainy season and were used by shepherds and travellers. When empty they could be used for prisons.

JOSEPH IN EGYPT

And Joseph was brought down to Egypt; and Potiphar, an officer of Pharaoh, captain of the guard, an Egyptian, bought him of the hands of the Ishmeelites, which had brought him down thither.

And the Lord was with Joseph. And his master saw that the Lord was with him, and that the Lord made all that he did to prosper in his hand. And Joseph found grace in his sight: and he made him overseer over his house, and all that he had he put into his hand. And it came to pass from the time that he had made him overseer in his house, and over all that he had, that the Lord blessed the Egyptian's house for Joseph's sake; and the blessing of the Lord was upon all that he had in the house, and in the field.

And he left all that he had in Joseph's hand; and he knew not aught he had, save the bread which he did eat. And Joseph was a goodly person, and well favoured.

[Potiphar's wife tried to make Joseph unfaithful to his master. When she found that Joseph would not betray the trust shown to him by Potiphar, she told her husband lies about Joseph. Potiphar in his anger threw Joseph into prison.]

But the Lord was with Joseph, and shewed him mercy, and gave him favour in the sight of the keeper of the prison. And the keeper of the prison committed to Joseph's hand all the prisoners that were in the prison; and whatsoever they did there, he was the doer of it. Because the Lord was with him, and that which he did, the Lord made it to prosper.

Genesis xxxix.1-6, 21-23

*JOSEPH IN PRISON

And Pharaoh was wroth against the chief of the butlers, and against the chief of the bakers. And he put them into the prison where Joseph was.

And Joseph came in unto them in the morning, and looked upon them, and, behold, they were sad. And he asked, Wherefore look ye so sadly to day? And they said unto him, We have dreamed a dream, and there is no interpreter of it. And Joseph said unto them, Do not interpretations belong to God? Tell me them, I pray you.

THINGS THAT JOSEPH MAY HAVE
SEEN IN EGYPT

This picture from a drawing made at the time
shows slaves being sold in the slave-market.

The plough was a very poor tool
made of a few stakes. It merely
scratched a small groove in the
soil, and could only be used when
the earth was soft, that is, in the
winter and the spring.

The same kind of boat
which was used thou-
sands of years ago can
still be seen on the
River Nile today.

The heavy weight made
it easy to lift water from
the river and pour it
into ditches to water the
land.

And the chief butler said to him, In my dream, behold, a vine was before me; and in the vine were three branches: and it was as though it budded, and her blossoms shot forth; and the clusters thereof brought forth ripe grapes: And Pharaoh's cup was in my hand: and I took the grapes, and pressed them into Pharaoh's cup, and I gave the cup into Pharaoh's hand. And Joseph said unto him, This is the interpretation of it: The three branches are three days. Yet within three days shall Pharaoh lift up thine head, and restore thee unto thy place.

Think on me when it shall be well with thee, and make mention of me unto Pharaoh, and bring me out of this house.

When the chief baker saw that the interpretation was good, he said unto Joseph, In my dream, behold, I had three white baskets on my head. And in the uppermost basket there was of all manner of bakemeats for Pharaoh; and the birds did eat them out of the basket upon my head. And Joseph answered and said, This is the interpretation thereof: The three baskets are three days. Yet within three days shall Pharaoh lift up thy head from off thee, and shall hang thee on a tree; and the birds shall eat thy flesh from off thee.

And it came to pass the third day, which was Pharaoh's birthday, that he made a feast unto all his servants. And he restored the chief butler unto his butlership again; and he gave the cup into Pharaoh's hand. But he hanged the chief baker: as Joseph had interpreted to them. Yet did not the chief butler remember Joseph, but forgat him.

Genesis xl

*JOSEPH IS MADE RULER

And it came to pass at the end of two years, that Pharaoh dreamed: and, behold, he stood by the river. And there came up out of the river seven fat-fleshed kine; and they fed in a meadow. And, behold, seven lean-fleshed kine came up after them out of the river. And the lean-fleshed kine did eat up the seven fat kine. So Pharaoh awoke.

And he slept and dreamed the second time: and, behold, seven ears of corn came up on one stalk, rank and good. And, behold, seven thin ears

The dream of the butler.

The dream of the baker.

Butler means cup-bearer. It was a very high office. The cup-bearer's duty was to guard against poison. He had to sip everything that the king was about to drink, to make sure that it was harmless.

The Egyptians embalmed the bodies of the dead so that they would have a body for life after death. The baker was horrified that his body would not be preserved.

Joseph as a slave (from a drawing made at the time).

21

sprung up after them. And the seven thin ears devoured the seven rank and full ears. And Pharaoh awoke.

And in the morning he sent for all the magicians of Egypt, and all the wise men thereof, and told them his dream; but there was none that could interpret them unto Pharaoh. Then spake the chief butler unto Pharaoh, saying, I do remember my faults this day: Pharaoh was wroth with his servants, and put me in ward, both me and the chief baker. And we dreamed a dream one night. And there was with us a young man, an Hebrew, and he interpreted to us our dreams. And it came to pass, as he interpreted to us, so it was.

Then Pharaoh sent and called Joseph. And Pharaoh said unto Joseph, I have dreamed a dream, and there is none that can interpret it. I have heard say of thee, that thou canst understand a dream to interpret it.

And Joseph answered Pharaoh, saying, It is not in me. God shall give Pharaoh an answer of peace.

And Joseph said unto Pharaoh, The dream of Pharaoh is one: God hath shewed Pharaoh what he is about to do. The seven good kine and the seven good ears are seven years. And the seven thin kine and the seven empty ears shall be seven years of famine. What God is about to do He sheweth unto Pharaoh. Behold, there come seven years of great plenty, and there shall arise after them seven years of famine; and all the plenty shall not be known in the land by reason of that famine following; for it shall be very grievous. And for that the dream was doubled unto Pharaoh twice; it is because the thing is established by God, and God will shortly bring it to pass. Now therefore let Pharaoh look out a man discreet and wise, and set him over the land of Egypt. And let him appoint officers over the land, and let them gather all the food of those good years that come, and lay up corn under the hand of Pharaoh, and let them keep food in the cities. And that food shall be for store against the seven years of famine, that the land perish not through the famine.

And the thing was good in the eyes of Pharaoh. And Pharaoh said unto Joseph, Forasmuch as God hath shewed thee all this, there is none so discreet and wise as thou art: according unto thy word shall all my people be ruled: only in the throne will I be greater than thou. See, I have set thee over the land of Egypt.

And Pharaoh took off his ring from his hand, and put it upon Joseph's hand, and arrayed him in fine linen, and put a gold chain about his neck; and he made him to ride in the second chariot which he had; and he made him ruler over all the land of Egypt.

Genesis xli

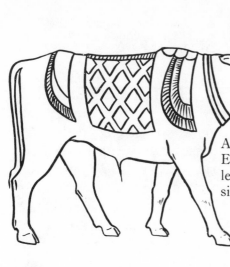

Egyptian

Phoenician

Early Greek

Later Greek

Apis, the bull, was a god in Egypt. It is said that our letter "A" comes from the sign for this god.

Egypt was one of the first countries where people stayed in one place to grow food instead of wandering with herds and flocks.

Great statues often had the head of a king or queen.

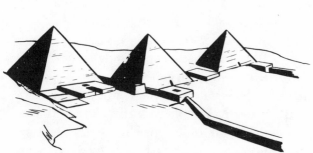

The pyramids were built before the time of Joseph, and he would have seen them. They are the tombs of Egyptian royalty.

The Egyptians had many gods. This is an emblem showing one of them, Osiris, holding up the sun which gives life to the world.

THE COMING OF HIS BRETHREN

[Famine was great in Egypt and in the surrounding countries and the people of these countries came to Joseph to buy corn. When Jacob learnt that there was corn to be had in Egypt he sent Joseph's ten elder brothers to buy corn.

Joseph knew his brothers but they did not recognize him. He called them spies and imprisoned them. They protested that they were not spies but simple shepherds from Canaan, and that they had left their aged father and younger brother there. Joseph told them that they could prove this to be true by leaving one of their number in prison, taking corn back to Canaan and returning with the younger brother. Simon was left in prison and the other brothers returned home with their sacks of corn. Unknown to them, Joseph had commanded that their money should be placed in each sack of corn.

When the corn had been eaten, Jacob again sent the brothers to Egypt—with presents to Joseph, the money that had been returned in the sacks and money to buy fresh supplies of corn. This time, much against Jacob's wish, Benjamin the youngest brother went with them.

Joseph greeted them and feasted them, making much of Benjamin, his young brother. Joseph ordered his servants to fill their sacks with corn, and to place in each sack the corn money, but in Benjamin's sack was to be placed Joseph's silver cup as well. Next morning, loading their asses with the sacks, the brothers departed. They had not gone many miles from the city when they were overtaken by Joseph's steward, who accused them of stealing his master's silver cup. A search was made, and the cup was found in Benjamin's sack. Greatly distressed, the party returned to the city and to Joseph. Joseph said that he would keep as a slave the brother in whose sack the cup had been found: the others could go. But the brothers pleaded that, if they returned to Canaan without Benjamin, their aged father, to whom Benjamin was very dear, would die of a broken heart.

Joseph then made himself known to them.

When Pharaoh learnt that Joseph's brothers had come, he was pleased and told Joseph to send to Canaan for Jacob and all his household, that they might live in comfort in Egypt. Joseph sent wagons and gifts as Pharaoh had commanded, and the brothers returned home.

Jacob at first would not believe that his son Joseph was alive and was the governor of Egypt, but when he saw wagons and gifts he believed and was overjoyed, and he cried out: "It is enough, Joseph my son is yet alive: I will go and see him before I die."]

Genesis xlii-xlv

This picture from a tomb in Egypt shows a vizier being given his badges of office—a ring, a tunic of fine linen and a gold chain. In fact, the same things that were given to Joseph.

A Granary

The Egyptians let people who had no food enter their country to buy corn. Today we say "Corn in Egypt", meaning "a plentiful supply."

The chariot which Pharaoh gave to Joseph may have looked like the one in this drawing. The drawing was found in an Egyptian temple.

*THE COMING OF THE ISRAELITES TO EGYPT

And God said, Jacob, Jacob. And he said, Here am I. And he said, I am God, the God of thy father. Fear not to go down into Egypt; for I will there make of thee a great nation: I will go down with thee into Egypt; and I will also surely bring thee up again. And Jacob rose up from Beer-sheba: and the sons carried Jacob their father, and their little ones, and their wives, in the wagons which Pharaoh had sent. And they took their cattle, and their goods, and came into Egypt, Jacob, and all his seed with him.

And they came into the land of Goshen. And Joseph made ready his chariot, and went up to meet his father, and presented himself unto him; and he fell on his neck, and wept on his neck a good while. And Joseph said unto his brethren, I will go up, and shew Pharaoh, and say unto him, My brethren, and my father's house, which were in the land of Canaan, are come unto me; and the men are shepherds, and they have brought their flocks, and their herds, and all that they have.

And when Pharaoh shall call you, and shall say, What is your occupation? ye shall say, Thy servants' trade hath been about cattle: that ye may dwell in the land of Goshen.

And it came to pass after these things, that one told Joseph, Behold, thy father is sick: and he took with him his two sons, Manasseh and Ephraim. And one told Jacob, and said, Behold, thy son Joseph cometh. And Jacob strengthened himself and sat upon the bed. And Jacob said unto Joseph, God Almighty appeared unto me in the land of Canaan, and blessed me, and said unto me, Behold, I will make thee fruitful, and multiply thee, and will give this land to thy seed after thee for an everlasting possession.

When I came from Padan, Rachel died, when there was but a little way to come unto Ephrath: and I buried her there in the way of Ephrath; the same is Beth-lehem.

And Jacob beheld Joseph's sons, and said, Bring them, I pray thee, unto me, and I will bless them.

And Jacob called unto his sons, and said, Gather yourselves together, that I may tell you that which shall befall you in the last days.

And when Jacob had made an end of commanding his sons, he gathered up his feet into the bed, and yielded up the ghost, and was gathered unto his people.

Genesis xlvi.2-6, 28-34; xlviii.1-12; xlix.1, 33

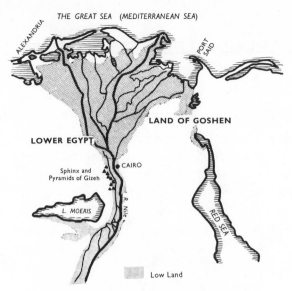

THE GREAT SEA (MEDITERRANEAN SEA)

ALEXANDRIA

PORT SAID

LAND OF GOSHEN

LOWER EGYPT

Sphinx and
Pyramids of Gizeh

CAIRO

R. Nile

L. MOERIS

RED SEA

Low Land

Goshen was where the Egyptians let the Hebrews settle.

An Ox Wagon
The Israelites had no wheeled transport. This is why Pharaoh told Joseph to send some to his family.

Egyptian money. The Egyptians used ring money. The coins were of silver and could be put on a cord for easy carrying.

Balm. This may have been the resin from the mastich tree which was very valuable and used for medicine.

Nuts. Pistachio nuts were liked very much. They were used for medicine. Today the nuts give the flavouring and colour to green ice-cream.

Spices. Today spices are used to flavour food. In Old Testament times they were plants which were heated to give sweet scents.

Honey. Probably not the honey we know but the syrup made from boiling grape-juice. The Israelites would not have sent honey to the Egyptians, who were themselves great bee-keepers.

SAND DWELLERS
The Egyptians did not think very highly of the Israelites, because they looked after cattle and sheep. They called them "sand dwellers".
The Egyptians had been conquered by the Hyskos, who were sand dwellers. Under these "Shepherd Kings" Joseph gained a rank he would not have had under an Egyptian ruler. This also was why the Israelites were made welcome.

*MOSES' CHILDHOOD—FLIGHT FROM EGYPT

And Pharaoh charged all his people, saying, Every son that is born ye shall cast into the river, and every daughter ye shall save alive. And there went a man of the house of Levi, and took to wife a daughter of Levi. The woman bare a son: and when she saw that he was a goodly child, she hid him three months. When she could not longer hide him, she took an ark of bulrushes, and daubed it with slime and with pitch, and put the child therein; and she laid it in the flags by the river's brink. His sister stood afar off.

The daughter of Pharaoh came down to wash herself at the river; and when she saw the ark among the flags, she sent her maid to fetch it. And when she had opened it, she saw the child: and, behold, the babe wept. And she had compassion on him, and said, This is one of the Hebrews' children. Then said his sister to Pharaoh's daughter, Shall I go and call a nurse of the Hebrew women, that she may nurse the child for thee? And Pharaoh's daughter said to her, Go. And the maid went and called the child's mother. And Pharaoh's daughter said unto her, Take this child away, and nurse it for me, and I will give thee thy wages. And the woman took the child, and nursed it

And the child grew, and she brought him unto Pharaoh's daughter, and he became her son. And she called his name Moses: and she said, Because I drew him out of the water.

It came to pass in those days, when Moses was grown, that he went unto his brethren, and looked on their burdens: and he spied an Egyptian smiting an Hebrew, one of his brethren. And he looked this way and that way, and when he saw that there was no man, he slew the Egyptian, and hid him in the sand. And when he went out the second day, behold, two men of the Hebrews strove together: and he said to him that did the wrong, Wherefore smitest thou thy fellow? And he said, Who made thee a prince and a judge over us? intendest thou to kill me, as thou killedst the Egyptian? And Moses feared, and said, Surely this thing is known.

Now when Pharaoh heard this thing, he sought to slay Moses. But Moses fled from the face of Pharaoh, and dwelt in the land of Midian.

It came to pass in process of time, that the king of Egypt died: and the children of Israel sighed by reason of the bondage, and they cried, and their cry came up unto God. And God heard their groaning, and God remembered his covenant with Abraham, with Isaac, and with Jacob.

Exodus i and ii

MOSES

The name *Moses* is made from two Egyptian words— *mo*, which means "water", and *uses*, which means "saved out of".

Moses grew up as an Egyptian prince. He was taught about the Egyptian gods, but remained true to the God of his real father and mother.

PAPYRUS
The Egyptians made paper from this plant, and from its name comes the word "paper"

THERMUTHIS
This may have been the name of the princess who found Moses.

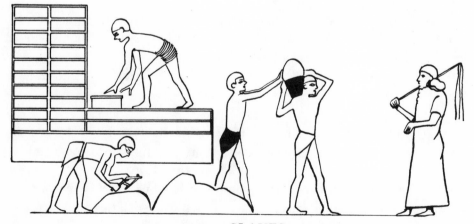

SLAVES
The Israelites had to make bricks, dig canals, and build houses.

*THE BURNING BUSH

Now Moses kept the flock of Jethro, the priest of Midian: and he led the flock to the desert, and came to the mountain of God. And the angel of the Lord appeared unto him in a flame of fire out of the midst of a bush: and he looked, and the bush burned with fire, and the bush was not consumed. And Moses said, I will now turn aside, and see this great sight, why the bush is not burnt. And when the Lord saw that he turned aside to see, God called unto him, and said, Draw not hither: put off thy shoes, for the place whereon thou standest is holy ground. I am the God of thy father, the God of Abraham, the God of Isaac, and the God of Jacob. And Moses hid his face; for he was afraid to look upon God.

And the Lord said, I have surely seen the afflictions of my people which are in Egypt, and I am come down to deliver them out of the hand of the Egyptians, and to bring them up out of that land unto a good land flowing with milk and honey. Come now, and I will send thee unto Pharaoh, that thou mayest bring forth my people the children of Israel out of Egypt.

And Moses said unto God, Who am I, that I should bring forth the children of Israel out of Egypt? And God said unto Moses: Go, and gather the elders of Israel together, and say unto them, The Lord God of your fathers appeared unto me, saying, I have surely visited you, and seen that which is done to you in Egypt: And I have said, I will bring you up out of the affliction of Egypt, unto a land flowing with milk and honey. And they shall hearken to thy voice: and thou shalt come unto the king of Egypt, and ye shall say unto him, The Lord God of the Hebrews hath met us. Now let us go three days' journey into the wilderness, that we may sacrifice to the Lord our God. And I am sure that the king of Egypt will not let you go. And I will stretch out my hand, and smite Egypt with all my wonders: after that he will let you go.

Exodus iii

MOSES IS GIVEN PROOF

[Moses said, "They will not believe me, and will say, I have not seen the Lord."

The Lord said, "Take the rod in thy hand and cast it on the ground." When Moses did so it became a serpent. Then the Lord said, "Take the serpent by the tail." Moses did so, and it once more became a rod.

Then the Lord said, "Put your hand inside your shirt." Moses did so. When he withdrew his hand it was white with leprosy. The Lord then told him to repeat the action.

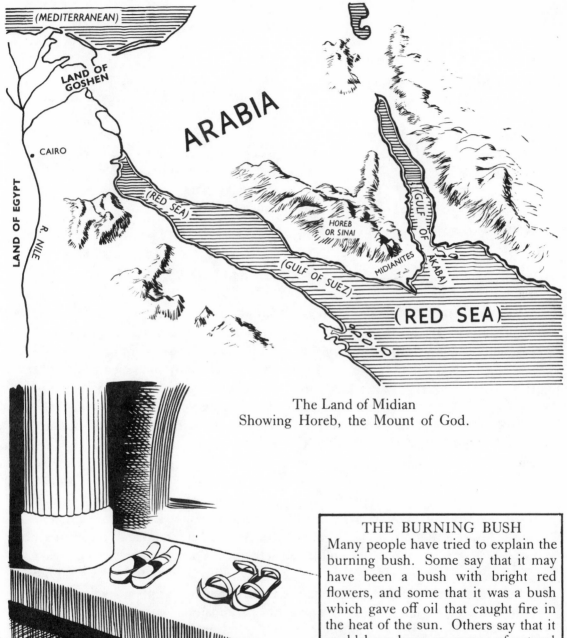

The Land of Midian
Showing Horeb, the Mount of God.

THE BURNING BUSH

Many people have tried to explain the burning bush. Some say that it may have been a bush with bright red flowers, and some that it was a bush which gave off oil that caught fire in the heat of the sun. Others say that it could have been an escape of natural gas from the ground.

Many people, however, believe that it was a miracle worked by God.

OUTSIDE A MOSQUE

Eastern peoples still take off their shoes when they enter a holy place. Shoes can be seen at the entrance to a mosque, or Mohammedan church.

31

When he took his hand out the second time it was clean and whole again.

Then the Lord said, "If the people do not believe these signs, then shall you take the water from the river and pour it over the dry land, and it shall become blood."

Moses then said to the Lord, "I am slow of speech and slow of tongue. How shall I speak to the people?"

The Lord answered, "I will be with thy mouth and with the mouth of thy brother, Aaron, and he shall be thy spokesman."

Moses then left Midian with his wife and sons, and journeyed to Egypt. When he showed the people the signs they believed in him and prayed to the Lord.]

Exodus iv

IN EGYPT

And the Lord said unto Moses, See, I have made thee a god to Pharaoh: and Aaron thy brother shall be thy prophet. Thou shalt speak all that I command thee: and Aaron thy brother shall speak unto Pharaoh, that he send the children of Israel out of his land. And I will harden Pharaoh's heart, and multiply my signs and my wonders in the land of Egypt. But Pharaoh shall not hearken unto you, that I may lay my hand upon Egypt, and bring forth mine armies, and my people the children of Israel, out of the land of Egypt by great judgments. And the Egyptians shall know that I am the Lord, when I stretch forth mine hand upon Egypt, and bring out the children of Israel from among them.

And Moses and Aaron did as the Lord commanded them, so did they. And Moses was fourscore years old, and Aaron fourscore and three years old, when they spake unto Pharaoh.

And the Lord spake unto Moses and unto Aaron, saying, When Pharaoh shall speak unto you, saying, Shew a miracle for you: then thou shalt say unto Aaron, Take thy rod, and cast it before Pharaoh, and it shall become a serpent.

And Moses and Aaron went in unto Pharaoh, and they did so as the Lord had commanded: and Aaron cast down his rod before Pharaoh, and before his servants, and it became a serpent. Then Pharaoh also called the wise men and the sorcerers: now the magicians of Egypt, they also did in like manner with their enchantments. For they cast down every man his rod, and they became serpents: but Aaron's rod swallowed up their rods. And he hardened Pharaoh's heart, that he hearkened not unto them; as the Lord had said.

Exodus vii.1-13

MOSES AND AARON BEFORE PHARAOH

The "wise men" were conjurors, the "sorcerers" spoke magic words, and the "magicians" kept the sacred books.

PROPHET

Moses was the *prophet* of God. He spoke the words which he received from God.

Moses could not speak well, and so his brother Aaron spoke for him.

*GOING OUT OF EGYPT

And the Lord spake unto Moses and Aaron, saying, This month shall be the first month of the year to you. Speak ye unto all Israel saying, In the tenth day of this month they shall take every man a lamb. Your lamb shall be without blemish, a male of the first year: ye shall take it from the sheep, or from the goats. And ye shall keep it until the fourteenth day: and the whole assembly of Israel shall kill it in the evening. And they shall take of the blood, and strike it on the two side posts and on the upper door post of the houses. And they shall eat the flesh in that night, roast with fire, and unleavened bread; and with bitter herbs. And thus shall ye eat it; with your loins girded, your shoes on your feet, and your staff in your hand; It is the Lord's passover.

And it came to pass, when Pharaoh had let the people go, that God led them not through the land of the Philistines; for God said, Lest the people repent when they see war, and return to Egypt: But God led the people through the wilderness of the Red Sea. And the Lord went before them by day in a pillar of a cloud, to lead them the way; and by night in a pillar of fire, to give them light.

And the heart of Pharaoh and of his servants was turned against the people, and they said, Why have we let Israel go from serving us? And he made ready his chariot and took his people with him.

And when Pharaoh drew nigh, the children of Israel cried out unto the Lord. And Moses said unto the people, Fear ye not, stand still, and see the salvation of the Lord. The Lord shall fight for you. And the Lord said unto Moses, Lift up thy rod, and stretch out thine hand over the sea, and divide it: and the children of Israel shall go on dry ground through the midst of the sea. And Moses stretched out his hand; and the Lord caused the sea to go back by a strong east wind all that night, and made the sea dry land. And the children of Israel went into the midst of the sea upon the dry ground.

And the Egyptians went in after them. And the Lord said unto Moses, Stretch out thine hand over the sea, that the waters may come again upon the Egyptians, upon their chariots, and upon their horsemen. And Moses stretched forth his hand, and the waters returned, and covered all the chariots, and all the host of Pharaoh. Thus the Lord saved Israel that day out of the hand of the Egyptians.

And Miriam the prophetess, the sister of Aaron, took a timbrel in her hand; and all the women went out after her with timbrels and with dances. And Miriam answered them, Sing ye to the Lord, for he hath triumphed gloriously.

So Moses brought Israel from the Red Sea and they went out into the wilderness of Shur; and they went three days and found no water. And when they came to Marah, they could not drink of the waters, for they were bitter. And the people murmured against Moses, saying, What shall we drink? And he cried unto the Lord; and the Lord shewed him a tree, which when he had cast into the waters, the waters were made sweet.

And they came to Elim, where were twelve wells, and threescore and ten palm trees: and they encamped there by the waters.

Exodus xii.1-11, xiii.17-22, xiv, xv.20-27

FEAST OF THE PASSOVER

Jews still hold the Feast of the Passover. The table is known as the *Seder Table*.

A special bread called *Matzot* is eaten with
   Roast lamb—this stands for the lamb whose blood was smeared on the doorposts.
   Hard-boiled egg—this means a festival.
   Wine—always from Palestine.

On the table an extra cup of wine is placed, known as *Elijah's Cup*. This is kept for an unexpected visitor.

A custom of the feast is to hide a piece of *Matzot*. The children look for it, and the finder can have any gift he wants.

*IN THE WILDERNESS

And they took their journey from Elim, and came unto the wilderness of Sin. And the whole congregation of the children of Israel murmured against Moses and Aaron, and said unto them, Would to God we had died by the hand of the Lord in Egypt, when we sat by the flesh pots, and did eat bread to the full; for ye have brought us forth into this wilderness, to kill this whole assembly with hunger.

Then said the Lord unto Moses, Behold, I will rain bread from heaven for you; and the people shall go out and gather a certain rate every day, that I may prove them, whether they will walk in my law, or no. And it shall come to pass, that on the sixth day they shall prepare that which they bring in; and it shall be twice as much as they gather daily. At even ye shall eat flesh, and in the morning ye shall be filled with bread; and ye shall know that I am the Lord your God.

And it came to pass, that at even the quails came up, and covered the camp: and in the morning the dew lay round about. And when the dew was gone, there lay a small round thing, as small as the hoar frost on the ground. And when the children of Israel saw it, they said, It is manna: for they wist not what it was. And Moses said unto them, This is the bread which the Lord hath given you to eat. Gather of it, an omer for every man. And the children of Israel did so, and gathered, some more, some less.

And Moses said, Let no man leave of it till the morning. They hearkened not unto Moses; but some of them left of it until the morning, and it bred worms, and stank: and Moses was wroth with them. And they gathered it every morning: and when the sun waxed hot, it melted.

And it came to pass, that on the sixth day they gathered twice as much bread: and all the rulers of the congregation came and told Moses. And he said unto them, To morrow is the rest of the holy sabbath unto the Lord: bake that which ye will bake to day; and that which remaineth over lay up to be kept until the morning. And they laid it up as Moses bade: and it did not stink, neither was there any worm therein. So the people rested on the seventh day. And the house of Israel called the name thereof Manna: and it was like coriander seed, white; and the taste of it was like wafers made with honey.

And the children of Israel did eat manna forty years, until they came unto the borders of the land of Canaan.

And Jethro, Moses' father in law, came with his sons and his wife unto Moses in the wilderness, where he encamped at the mount of God. And Moses told his father in law all that the Lord had done unto Pharaoh and to the Egyptians for Israel's sake, and how the Lord delivered them. And Jethro rejoiced for all the goodness which the Lord had done to Israel.

And it came to pass on the morrow, that Moses sat to judge the people: and the people stood by Moses from the morning unto the evening. And when Moses' father in law saw all that he did, he said, What is this thing that thou doest to the people? And Moses said, the people come unto me to inquire of God: When they have a matter, they come unto me; and I judge between one and another.

And Moses' father in law said unto him, The thing that thou doest is not good. Thou wilt surely wear away, both thou, and this people that is with thee. I will give thee counsel. Provide out of all the people able men, such as fear God, men of truth; and place such over them, to be rulers of thousands, and rulers of hundreds, rulers of fifties, and rulers of tens. And let them judge the people at all seasons. So Moses hearkened to the voice of his father in law, and chose able men out of all Israel. And they judged the people at all seasons: the hard causes they brought unto Moses, but every small matter they judged themselves.

And Moses let his father in law depart; and he went his way into his own land.

Exodus xvi and xviii

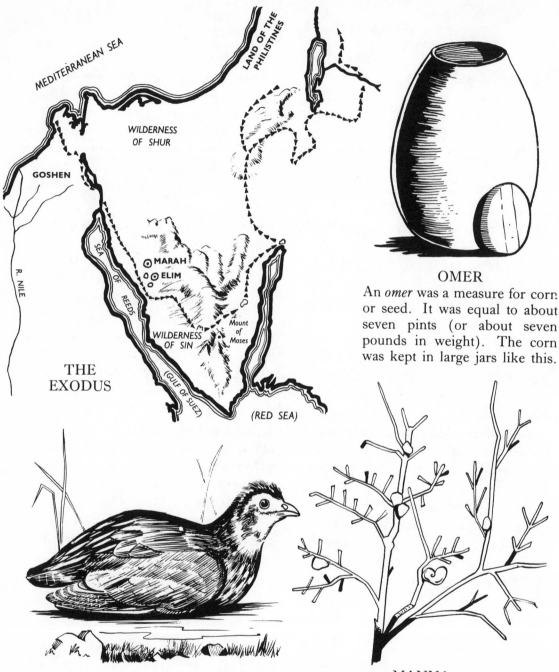

MEDITERRANEAN SEA

LAND OF THE PHILISTINES

WILDERNESS
OF SHUR

GOSHEN

R. NILE

SEA OF REEDS

⊙ MARAH
⊙ ELIM

WILDERNESS
OF SIN

Mount
of
Moses

(GULF OF SUEZ)

(RED SEA)

THE
EXODUS

OMER

An *omer* was a measure for corn
or seed. It was equal to about
seven pints (or about seven
pounds in weight). The corn
was kept in large jars like this.

QUAILS

These birds are about the size of a pigeon,
and brown in colour. They migrate from
Africa to eastern Europe. After crossing
the Red Sea they land and rest. They are
so tired that they can be caught by hand.

MANNA

This may have been the juice from the
tamarisk tree. To-day the Bedouin collect
the white juice which drips from this tree.
Sometimes as much as four pounds can be
collected in a morning.

MOUNT SINAI

And the Lord said unto Moses, Come up to me into the mount, and be there: and I will give thee tables of stone, and a law, and commandments which I have written; that thou mayest teach them. And Moses rose up, and his minister Joshua: and Moses went up into the mount of God. And he said unto the elders, Tarry ye here for us, until we come again unto you: and, behold Aaron and Hur are with you: if any man have any matters to do, let him come unto them.

And Moses went up into the mount, and a cloud covered the mount. And the glory of the Lord abode upon mount Sinai, and the cloud covered it six days: and the seventh day he called unto Moses out of the midst of the cloud. And the sight of the glory of the Lord was like devouring fire on the top of the mount in the eyes of the children of Israel. And Moses went into the midst of the cloud, and gat him up into the mount: and Moses was in the mount forty days and forty nights.

And · God spake all these words, saying, I am the Lord thy God, which have brought thee out of the land of Egypt, out of the house of bondage.

Thou shalt have no other gods before me.

Thou shalt not make unto thee any graven image, or any likeness of any thing that is in heaven above, or that is in the earth beneath, or that is in the water under the earth: Thou shalt not bow down thyself to them, nor serve them: for I the Lord thy God am a jealous God, visiting the iniquity of the fathers upon the children unto the third and fourth generation of them that hate me; And shewing mercy unto thousands of them that love me, and keep my commandments.

Thou shalt not take the name of the Lord thy God in vain; for the Lord will not hold him guiltless that taketh his name in vain.

Remember the sabbath day, to keep it holy. Six days shalt thou labour, and do all thy work: But the seventh day is the sabbath of the Lord thy God: in it thou shalt not do any work, thou, nor thy son, nor thy daughter, thy manservant, nor thy maidservant, nor thy cattle, nor thy stranger that is within thy gates: For in six days the Lord made heaven and earth, the sea, and all that in them is, and rested the seventh day: wherefor the Lord blessed the sabbath day, and hallowed it.

Honour thy father and thy mother: that thy days may be long upon the land which the Lord thy God giveth thee.

Thou shalt not kill.

Thou shalt not commit adultery.

Thou shalt not steal.

Thou shalt not bear false witness against thy neighbour.

Thou shalt not covet thy neighbour's house, thou shalt not covet thy neighbour's wife, nor his manservant, nor his maidservant, nor his ox, nor his ass, nor any thing that is thy neighbour's.

And all the people saw the thunderings, and the lightnings, and the noise of the trumpet, and the mountain smoking: and when the people saw it, they removed, and stood afar off.

Exodus xxiv.12-18, xx.1-18

THE FOURTH COMMANDMENT

A Jew may not even carry a parcel on the Sabbath. This would be called work.

A GRAVEN IMAGE

This is the kind of graven image that is spoken of in the Second Commandment. It was found in a grave over 2000 years old.

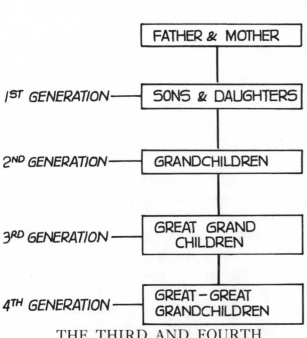

FATHER & MOTHER

1ST GENERATION —— SONS & DAUGHTERS

2ND GENERATION —— GRANDCHILDREN

3RD GENERATION —— GREAT GRAND CHILDREN

4TH GENERATION —— GREAT – GREAT GRANDCHILDREN

THE THIRD AND FOURTH GENERATIONS

This diagram shows in a simple form what is meant by the "third and fourth generations".

DEVOURING FIRE
on the top of the mount.

THE PROMISED LAND

All the commandments which I command thee this day shall ye observe to do, that ye may live, and multiply, and go in and possess the land which the Lord sware unto your fathers. And thou shalt remember all the way which the Lord thy God led thee these forty years in the wilderness, to humble thee, and to prove thee, to know what was in thine heart, whether thou wouldest keep his commandments, or no. And he humbled thee, and suffered thee to hunger, and fed thee with manna, which thou knewest not, neither did thy fathers know; that he might make thee know that man doth not live by bread only, but by every word that proceedeth out of the mouth of the Lord doth man live. Thy raiment waxed not old upon thee, neither did thy foot swell, these forty years. Thou shalt also consider in thine heart, that, as a man chasteneth his son, so the Lord thy God chasteneth thee. Therefore thou shalt keep the commandments of the Lord thy God, to walk in his ways, and to fear him.

For the Lord thy God bringeth thee into a good land, a land of brooks of water, of fountains and depths that spring out of valleys and hills; A land of wheat, and barley, and vines, and fig trees, and pomegranates; a land of oil olive, and honey; A land wherein thou shalt eat bread without scarceness, thou shalt not lack any thing in it; a land whose stones are iron, and out of whose hills thou mayest dig brass.

When thou hast eaten and art full, then thou shalt bless the Lord thy God for the good land which he hath given thee. Beware that thou forget not the Lord thy God, in not keeping his commandments, and his judgments, and his statutes, which I command thee this day: Lest when thou hast eaten and art full, and hast built goodly houses, and dwelt therein; And when thy herds and thy flocks multiply, and thy silver and thy gold is multiplied, and all that thou hast is multiplied; Then thine heart be lifted up, and thou forget the Lord thy God, which brought thee forth out of the land of Egypt, from the house of bondage.

Deuteronomy viii.1-14

BROOKS
These were streams of running water that never dried up.

FOUNTAINS
Springs that always flowed.

HONEY
from the hives.

LAND OF MILK AND HONEY

**IRON and
COPPER MINES**
(Brass)

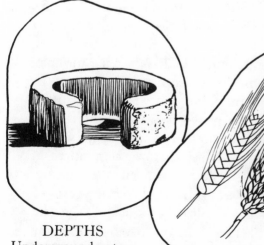

DEPTHS
Underground waters reached by a well.

BARLEY and WHEAT

**VINES, FIGS,
POMEGRANATES**

*DEBORAH
HEROINE AND LIBERATOR

And the children of Israel again did evil in the sight of the Lord, and the Lord sold them into the hand of Jabin king of Canaan, the captain of whose host was Sisera. And the children of Israel cried unto the Lord.

And Deborah, a prophetess, judged Israel at that time: and the children of Israel came up to her for judgment.

And she sent and called Barak, and said unto him, Hath not the Lord God of Israel commanded, saying, Go and draw toward mount Tabor, and take with thee ten thousand men? I will draw unto thee to the river Kishon Sisera, the captain of Jabin's army, with his chariots and his multitude; and I will deliver him into thine hand.

And Barak went up with ten thousand men: and Deborah went up with him. And Sisera gathered together all his chariots, even nine hundred chariots of iron, and all the people that were with him. And Deborah said unto Barak, This is the day in which the Lord hath delivered Sisera into thine hand. So Barak went down from mount Tabor, and ten thousand men after him. And the Lord discomfited Sisera, and all his chariots, and all his host; so that Sisera lighted down off his chariot, and fled away on his feet. But Barak pursued after the chariots, and all the host of Sisera fell upon the edge of the sword; and there was not a man left. Sisera fled to the tent of Jael the wife of Heber the Kenite.

And Jael went out to meet Sisera, and said unto him, Fear not. And when he had turned into the tent, she covered him with a mantle. And he said unto her, Give me, I pray thee, a little water to drink; for I am thirsty. And she opened a bottle of milk, and gave him drink, and covered him. Again he said unto her, Stand in the door of the tent, and when any man doth say, Is there any man here? thou shalt say, No.

Then Jael took a nail of the tent, and took an hammer in her hand, and went softly unto him, and smote the nail into his temples, and fastened it into the ground: for he was fast asleep and weary. So he died. And, as Barak pursued Sisera, Jael came out to meet him, and said unto him, Come, and I will shew thee the man whom thou seekest. And when he came into her tent, Sisera lay dead, and the nail was in his temples. So God subdued on that day Jabin the king of Canaan before the children of Israel. And the hand of the children of Israel prospered, and prevailed against Jabin the king of Canaan, until they had destroyed Jabin king of Canaan.

Judges iv

CHARIOTS OF IRON

This is a picture of an Assyrian royal chariot. Canaanite chariots would be like this, but simpler.

The Israelites settled in the mountains, because the Canaanites with their chariots of iron were able to defeat them in battle. Chariots were the tanks of olden times. They were of wood covered with iron. They held three men—a driver, a bowman, and a shield-bearer.

In the battle against Sisera, the Lord sent a shower of hail into the faces of the Canaanites. Their heavy iron chariots were stuck in the mud and could not move.

NAIL
The nail used by Jael was
a large wooden tent-peg.

BOTTLE
The bottle of milk would have been a
bag of leather holding sour milk.

RUTH AND NAOMI

[Once when there was a great famine, a man called Elimelech, with his wife Naomi and their two sons, left Beth-lehem-judah and went to live in the land of Moab. The father and the two sons died, and Naomi was left with her two daughters in law, Ruth and Orpah. When she had heard that the famine was over she decided to return to her own land, and urged Ruth and Orpah to return to their own families. Orpah did so, but Ruth said that she would never leave Naomi, that wherever Naomi went she would go as well, that her husband's people would be her people and his gods would be her gods.

When they returned to Beth-lehem-judah, Naomi and Ruth were very poor, and the only food they could get was the corn that the reapers had left behind as they harvested. Poor people were allowed to collect this corn and keep it for themselves. The field in which Ruth worked was owned by a rich relation of Naomi's, called Boaz. When he saw Ruth he called her and said, "Stay in my field and glean behind my reapers. I have been told how you have left your own land to look after your mother-in-law, Naomi."

Boaz gave instructions that Ruth was to eat at his table, and when she arose to start work he secretly told his reapers that they were not to mind if she searched for corn among the sheaves, and that they should leave some corn behind on purpose, so that Ruth would have plenty to glean. When the evening came, Ruth had collected an ephah of barley. Ruth stayed and gleaned with the reapers of Boaz for the whole of the barley harvest and the wheat harvest.

Later Boaz married Ruth, and she had a baby son called Obed. The women of the village were very happy for Naomi, and they said, "The Lord has looked after you. Now you have a kinsman who shall be famous in Israel, and who will look after you in your old age, for he is the son of your daughter in law Ruth, who has cared for you better than seven sons."

What the women said came true, for the baby grew up to be the grandfather of David.]

Ruth i; ii; iv.13-17

46

GLEANERS

The poor of the village were allowed to glean or collect the corn which had been missed by the reapers and left on the ground.

RUTH

Ruth carried home an ephah of corn (about a bushel) in her veil. This was a heavy cloak worn over head and shoulders.

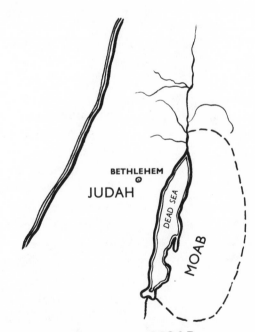

MOAB

Moab was only about a hundred miles from Bethlehem, but Ruth was a foreigner with different customs and gods.

*THE BIRTH OF SAMUEL AND EARLY DAYS IN THE TEMPLE

Hannah rose and prayed unto the Lord. She vowed a vow, and said, O Lord of hosts, if thou wilt not forget thine handmaid, but wilt give unto thine handmaid a man child, then I will give him unto the Lord all the days of his life.

Wherefore it came to pass, that she bare a son, and called his name Samuel, saying, Because I have asked him of the Lord.

And when she had weaned him, she took him up with her, with three bullocks, and one ephah of flour, and a bottle of wine, and brought him unto the house of the Lord in Shiloh: and the child was young. And they slew a bullock, and brought the child to Eli. And she said, Oh my lord, I am the woman that stood by thee here, praying unto the Lord. For this child I prayed; and the Lord hath given me my petition. Therefore also I have lent him to the Lord; as long as he liveth he shall be lent to the Lord.

Now the sons of Eli knew not the Lord. But Samuel ministered before the Lord, being a child, girded with a linen ephod. Moreover his mother made him a little coat, and brought it to him from year to year, when she came up with her husband to offer the yearly sacrifice.

Now Eli was very old, and heard all that his sons did. And he said unto them, Why do ye such things? for I hear of your evil dealings.

And there came a man of God unto Eli, and said unto him, Thus saith the Lord, Them that honour me I will honour, and they that despise me shall be lightly esteemed. And this shall be a sign unto thee, that shall come upon thy two sons, Hophni and Phinehas; in one day they shall die both of them. And I will raise up a faithful priest, that shall do according to that which is in mine heart: and I will build him a sure house; and he shall walk before mine anointed for ever.

1 Samuel i.9-28; ii.12-35

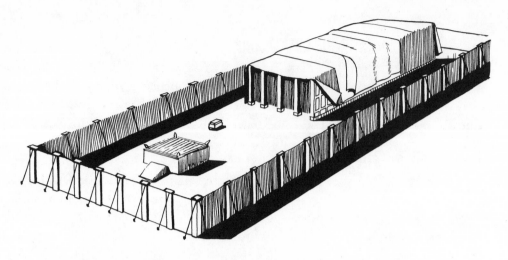

THE HOUSE OF THE LORD
(TABERNACLE)

At this time the House of the Lord was made of wood and richly decorated cloth. The Ark was kept in it. In the courtyard was the Altar of Burnt Offering. Eli was a High Priest.

AN EPHOD
A simple tunic worn by a priest. The "little coat" was an ephod.

AN EPHAH
An ephah of flour was about one-and-an-eighth bushels. In our weights, this is about 60 pounds.

SHILOH
Shiloh was the resting-place which Joshua chose for the Ark of the Covenant, after he had conquered most of the land of Canaan. He cast lots in front of the Ark, to decide which parts of Canaan each tribe should have.

*THE LORD'S VOICE

And the child Samuel ministered unto the Lord before Eli. And it came to pass at that time, when Eli was laid down in his place, and his eyes began to wax dim, that he could not see; and ere the lamp of God went out in the temple of the Lord, where the ark of God was, and Samuel was laid down to sleep; that the Lord called Samuel: and he answered, Here am I.

He ran to Eli, and said, Here am I; for thou calledst me. And he said, I called not; lie down again. And the Lord called yet again, Samuel. And Samuel arose and went to Eli, and said, Here am I; for thou didst call me. He answered, I called not, my son; lie down again. And the Lord called Samuel again the third time. He arose and went to Eli, and said, Here am I; for thou didst call me. And Eli perceived that the Lord had called the child.

Eli said unto Samuel, Go, lie down: and it shall be, if he call thee, that thou shalt say, Speak, Lord; for thy servant heareth. So Samuel went and lay down in his place. And the Lord came, and called, Samuel, Samuel.

Then Samuel answered, Speak; for thy servant heareth.

The Lord said to Samuel, Behold, I will do a thing in Israel, at which both the ears of every one that heareth it shall tingle. In that day I will perform against Eli all things which I have spoken concerning his house. For I have told him that I will judge his house for ever; because his sons made themselves vile, and he restrained them not.

And Samuel lay until the morning, and opened the doors of the house of the Lord. And Samuel feared to shew Eli the vision. Then Eli called Samuel, Samuel, my son, what is the thing that the Lord hath said unto thee? I pray thee hide it not from me. And Samuel told him, and hid nothing from him. And he said, It is the Lord: let him do what seemeth him good.

Samuel grew, and the Lord was with him, and did let none of his words fall to the ground. And all Israel from Dan even to Beer-sheba knew that Samuel was to be a prophet of the Lord.

1 Samuel iii.1-20

THE LAMP

As fire was difficult to make, it became customary to keep a lamp always burning.

THE ARK OF THE COVENANT

In it were the two stones given by God to Moses. The Ark was taken into battle by the sons of Eli, and captured by the Philistines. This was the meaning of God's words to Samuel, "I will do a thing in Israel, at which both the ears of every one that heareth it shall tingle."

No one knows the exact shape of the Ark. It may have looked like this, or like the one shown in Book Two.

A JEWISH HIGH PRIEST

*SAUL IS CHOSEN

There was a man of Benjamin, whose name was Kish. He had a son, whose name was Saul: and there was not among the children of Israel a goodlier person than he. And the asses of Kish were lost. Kish said to Saul, Take one of the servants with thee, and go seek the asses. And he passed through mount Ephraim, the land of Shalisha, the land of Shalim, and the land of the Benjamites, but they found them not. When they were come to the land of Zuph, Saul said to his servant, Come, let us return; lest my father take thought for us. And he said unto him, There is in this city a man of God; peradventure he can shew us our way that we should go. Then said Saul, But if we go, what shall we bring the man? The servant answered, I have the fourth part of a shekel of silver. Then said Saul, Well said, come, let us go. So they went unto the city where the man of God was.

Now the Lord had told Samuel a day before Saul came, saying, To morrow about this time I will send thee a man out of the land of Benjamin, and thou shalt anoint him to be captain over my people Israel, that he may save my people out of the hand of the Philistines. When Samuel saw Saul, the Lord said unto him, Behold the man whom I spake to thee of!

Then Saul drew near to Samuel and said, Tell me, I pray thee, where the seer's house is. Samuel answered, I am the seer: go before me unto the high place; for ye shall eat with me to day. As for thine asses, they are found. And on whom is all the desire of Israel? Is it not on thee, and on all thy father's house? Saul answered, Am not I a Benjamite, of the smallest of the tribes of Israel? Wherefore then speakest thou so to me?

And Samuel took Saul and his servant, and made them sit in the chiefest place among them that were bidden.

And when they were come down from the high place into the city, Samuel communed with Saul upon the top of the house. And they arose early: and as they were going down to the end of the city, Samuel said to Saul, Bid the servant pass on before us, but stand thou still a while, that I may shew thee the word of God.

Then Samuel took a vial of oil, and poured it upon his head, and kissed him, and said, The Lord hath anointed thee to be captain over his inheritance.

And Samuel called the people together, and said unto the children of Israel, Thus saith the Lord God of Israel, I brought up Israel out of Egypt, and delivered you out of the hand of the Egyptians, and out of the hand of them that oppressed you. Ye have this day rejected your God, and ye have said unto him, Nay, but set a king over us. Now therefore present yourselves before the Lord by your tribes, and by your thousands.

When Samuel had caused all the tribes of Israel to come near, he said to all the people, See ye him whom the Lord hath chosen, that there is none like him among all the people? All the people shouted, and said, God save the king.

1 Samuel ix, x

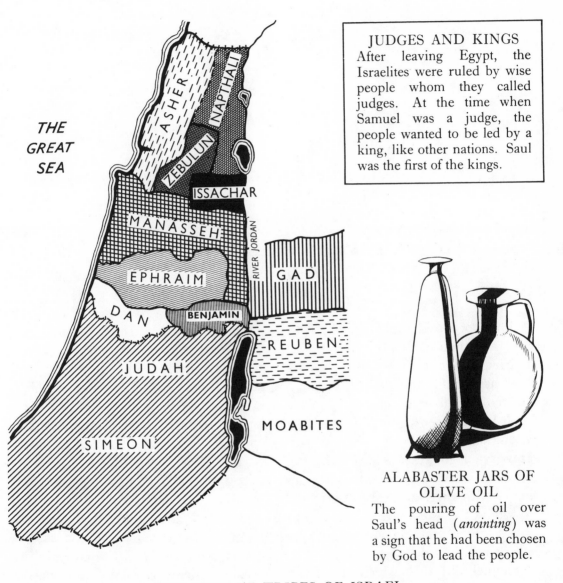

THE GREAT SEA

ASHER
NAPTHALI
ZEBULUN
ISSACHAR
MANASSEH
RIVER JORDAN
EPHRAIM
GAD
DAN
BENJAMIN
REUBEN
JUDAH
MOABITES
SIMEON

JUDGES AND KINGS

After leaving Egypt, the Israelites were ruled by wise people whom they called judges. At the time when Samuel was a judge, the people wanted to be led by a king, like other nations. Saul was the first of the kings.

ALABASTER JARS OF OLIVE OIL

The pouring of oil over Saul's head (*anointing*) was a sign that he had been chosen by God to lead the people.

THE TWELVE TRIBES OF ISRAEL

Jacob had twelve sons. During the stay in Egypt the families of these sons had grown into tribes. When Jacob was dying, he blessed his sons and foretold their future (Genesis xlix).

When the Israelites conquered Canaan, they shared the land by drawing lots. The sons of Levi, being the priestly tribe, did not have a share of land. Joseph's two sons, Manasseh and Ephraim, each took a full tribe's share after their father's death.

*DAVID'S ANOINTMENT
AND INTRODUCTION TO SAUL

The Lord said unto Samuel, How long wilt thou mourn for Saul, seeing I have rejected him from reigning over Israel? fill thine horn with oil, and go, I will send thee to Jesse the Beth-lehemite: for I have provided me a king among his sons. Samuel said, How can I go? if Saul hear it he will kill me. The Lord said, Take an heifer with thee, and say, I am come to sacrifice to the Lord. Call Jesse to the sacrifice, and I will shew thee what thou shalt do.

Samuel did that which the Lord spake, and came to Beth-lehem. The elders of the town trembled, and said, Comest thou peaceably? He said, Peaceably: I am come to sacrifice unto the Lord: come with me to the sacrifice.

When they were come, he looked on Eliab, and said, Surely the Lord's anointed is before him. But the Lord said unto Samuel, Look not on his countenance, or on the height of his stature: for man looketh on the outward appearance, but the Lord looketh on the heart. Then Jesse called Abinadab, and made him pass before Samuel. He said, Neither hath the Lord chosen this. Then Jesse made Shammah to pass by, and he said, Neither hath the Lord chosen this.

Jesse made seven of his sons pass before Samuel. Samuel said, The Lord hath not chosen these. Are here all thy children? And he said, There remaineth yet the youngest, and he keepeth the sheep. Samuel said unto Jesse, Fetch him. And he sent, and

SHEPHERD'S PIPE

The shepherd made this, and played it to himself while he watched the sheep. He also used it as a call to the sheep.

THE HARP

The harp used by David was probably a lyre. The frame was often made of cypress wood. There were ten strings, made of thin gut from sheep.

SHOPHAR

A trumpet of ram's horn. Priests blew on shophars to call the people to worship, and to sound the charge in battle.

VESSELS OF HORN

The horns of animals were used for carrying oil, wine, and water.

A bull's horn was a sign of strength. Kings were anointed with oil from a bull's horn, so that they would be strong.

brought him in. Now he was ruddy, and withal of a beautiful countenance. The Lord said, Arise, anoint him: for this is he. Then Samuel took the horn of oil, and anointed him: and the spirit of the Lord came upon David from that day forward.

But the spirit of the Lord departed from Saul, and an evil spirit from the Lord troubled him. And Saul's servants said, Let our lord command thy servants, to seek out a man, who is a cunning player on an harp: and when the evil spirit from God is upon thee, he shall play and thou shalt be well. Saul said, Provide me now a man that can play well, and bring him to me. Then one of the servants said, I have seen a son of Jesse the Bethlehemite, that is cunning in playing, and a comely person, and the Lord is with him.

Saul sent messengers unto Jesse, and said, Send me David thy son. Jesse took an ass laden with bread, and a bottle of wine, and a kid, and sent them by David unto Saul. David came to Saul and stood before him: and he loved him greatly; and he became his armourbearer. And it came to pass, when the evil spirit from God was upon Saul, that David played: so Saul was refreshed and was well.

1 Samuel xvi

DAVID—POET AND MUSICIAN

David wrote many fine poems which are to be found in the Book of Psalms.

PSALM 23

This is one of the most famous of all his psalms:

> The Lord is my shepherd; I shall not want.
> He maketh me to lie down in green pastures:
> He leadeth me beside the still waters.
> He restoreth my soul:
> He leadeth me in the paths of righteousness for his name's sake.
> Yea, though I walk through the valley of the shadow of death,
> I will fear no evil: for thou art with me;
> thy rod and thy staff they comfort me.
> Thou preparest a table before me in the presence of mine enemies:
> Thou anointest my head with oil; my cup runneth over.
> Surely goodness and mercy shall follow me all the days of my life:
> and I will dwell in the house of the Lord for ever.

The psalms of David have been set to many tunes. This one is called "Crimond".

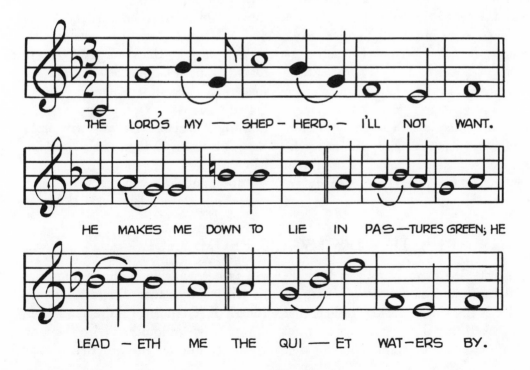

THE LORD'S MY SHEP-HERD,— I'LL NOT WANT.

HE MAKES ME DOWN TO LIE IN PAS—TURES GREEN; HE

LEAD—ETH ME THE QUI—ET WAT—ERS BY.

*JONATHAN AND SAUL'S JEALOUSY

Saul let him go no more home. Then Jonathan and David made a covenant, because he loved him. Jonathan stripped himself of the robe that was upon him, and gave it to David, and his garments, even to his sword, bow, and girdle. David behaved himself wisely, and Saul set him over the men of war, and he was accepted in the sight of the people, and in the sight of Saul's servants.

When David was returned from the slaughter of the Philistine, the women came out singing and dancing, and answered one another as they played, and said, Saul hath slain his thousands, and David his ten thousands. Saul was very wroth, and said, They have ascribed unto David ten thousands, and to me but thousands: what can he have more but the kingdom? And Saul eyed David from that day forward.

On the morrow, the evil spirit from God came upon Saul, and David played. There was a javelin in Saul's hand, and Saul cast the javelin; for he said, I will smite David. And David avoided out of his presence twice.

Saul was afraid of David. Therefore Saul removed him from him, and made him his captain over a thousand.

And Saul spake to Jonathan, and to his servants, that they should kill David. Jonathan told David, saying, Saul my father seeketh to kill thee: hide thyself. I will commune with my father of thee; and what I see, I will tell thee. And Jonathan spake good of David unto Saul his father. Saul hearkened unto Jonathan: and Saul sware, As the Lord liveth, he shall not be slain. Jonathan brought David to Saul, and he was in his presence, as in times past.

And there was war again: and David went out, and fought with the Philistines, and they fled from him. And the evil spirit from the Lord was upon Saul, as he sat with his javelin, and David played. Saul sought to smite David; but he slipped away and fled that night. Saul sent messengers to David's house to slay him in the morning. Michal, David's wife, told him, To morrow thou shalt be slain. Michal let David down through a window; and he escaped.

1 Samuel xviii.1-16; xix.1-12

*DAVID'S ESCAPE FROM SAUL

David fled from Naioth in Ramah, and came and said before Jonathan, What is my sin before thy father, that he seeketh my life? And he said unto him, God forbid; thou shalt not die: my father will do nothing, but that he will shew it me. David said unto Jonathan, To morrow is the new moon. To morrow I should sit with the king at meat: but let me go, that I may

BLOOD-BROTHER

It is a custom in many lands for men to swear everlasting friendship (a *covenant*) by cutting the wrists and exchanging blood.

The Israelites exchanged *clothes* to show friendship.

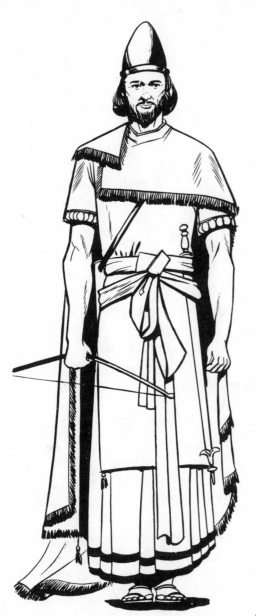

ROYAL DRESS

Jonathan, the eldest son of king Saul, would have worn clothes like this.

The girdle was of linen or leather, and was used to hold a sword and money.

THE SISTRUM

This was a rattle-like instrument, played by women at festivals.

Michal, David's wife, may have played one of these. Michal was the youngest daughter of Saul. David had to kill a hundred Philistines before he was allowed to marry her.

hide myself in the field unto the third day at even. If thy father miss me, then say, David asked leave that he might run to Beth-lehem: for there is a yearly sacrifice there for all the family. If he be very wroth, then be sure that evil is determined by him. Then said David, Who shall tell me? or what if thy father answer thee roughly?

Jonathan said unto David, If it please my father to do thee evil, then I will shew it thee. To morrow thou shalt be missed, because thy seat will be empty. When thou hast stayed three days, then shalt thou come down to the place where thou didst hide thyself. I will shoot three arrows, as though I shot at a mark, and I will send a lad, saying, Go, find the arrows. If I say, The arrows are on this side of thee, then come thou: for there is peace to thee. But if I say unto the young man, The arrows are beyond thee; go thy way, for the Lord hath sent thee away.

So David hid himself in the field: and when the new moon was come, the king sat down to eat meat, and David's place was empty. Saul spake not anything that day: for he thought, Something hath befallen him. And it came to pass on the morrow that David's place was empty: and Saul said unto Jonathan, Wherefore cometh not the son of Jesse to meat, neither yesterday, nor to day? Jonathan answered Saul, David asked leave of me to go to Beth-lehem. Therefore he cometh not unto the king's table. Then Saul's anger was kindled against Jonathan, and he said, For as long as the son of Jesse liveth, thou shalt not be established, nor thy kingdom. Send and fetch him unto me, for he shall surely die. Jonathan answered, What hath he done? And Saul cast a javelin at him, whereby Jonathan knew that it was determined of his father to slay David. So Jonathan arose from the table in fierce anger.

It came to pass in the morning, that Jonathan went out into the field, and a little lad with him. He said unto his lad, Run, find the arrows which I shoot. When the lad was come to the place of the arrow which Jonathan had shot, Jonathan cried, Is not the arrow beyond thee? Make speed, haste, stay not.

As soon as the lad was gone, David arose out of a place toward the south, fell on his face to the ground, and bowed himself three times: and they kissed one another and wept. Jonathan said unto David, Go in peace. The Lord be between me and thee, and between my seed and thy seed for ever. And he arose and departed: and Jonathan went into the city.

1 Samuel xx

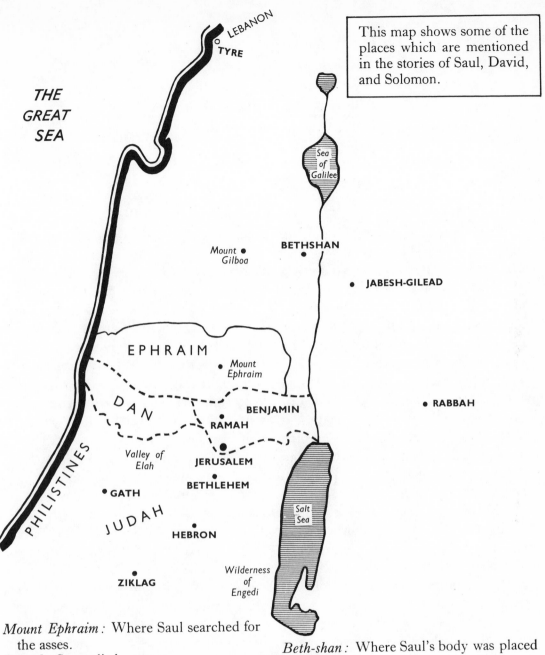

THE
GREAT
SEA

LEBANON

TYRE

Sea
of
Galilee

BETHSHAN

Mount
Gilboa

JABESH-GILEAD

This map shows some of the
places which are mentioned
in the stories of Saul, David,
and Solomon.

EPHRAIM

Mount
Ephraim

DAN

BENJAMIN

RABBAH

RAMAH

Valley of
Elah

JERUSALEM

BETHLEHEM

GATH

Salt
Sea

JUDAH

HEBRON

PHILISTINES

ZIKLAG

Wilderness
of
Engedi

Mount Ephraim: Where Saul searched for
the asses.

Ramah: Samuel's home.

Bethlehem: David's home.

Valley of Elah: Where David killed
Goliath.

Gath: Goliath's home.

Wilderness of Engedi: Where David found
Saul in a cave.

Ziklag: Where the Amalekites were
killed.

Mount Gilboa: Where Saul was killed.

Beth-shan: Where Saul's body was placed
on a wall.

Jabesh-Gilead: Where Saul's body was
burned.

Jerusalem: The city of king David.

Hebron: Where Abraham was buried.

Tyre: The capital city of king Hiram.

Lebanon: Where the cedar trees came
from.

Rabbah: Where Uriah the Hittite was
killed.

*SPARING SAUL'S LIFE

When Saul was returned from following the Philistines, it was told him, saying, David is in the wilderness of En-gedi. Saul took three thousand men, and went to seek David and his men upon the rocks of the wild goats. He came to the sheepcotes by the way, where was a cave: and Saul went in to cover his feet: and David and his men remained in the sides of the cave. The men of David said unto him, Behold the day of which the Lord said, Behold, I will deliver thine enemy into thine hand. Then David arose and cut off the skirt of Saul's robe. It came to pass afterwards, that David's heart smote him. He said unto his men, The Lord forbid that I should do this thing unto my master, the Lord's anointed, to stretch forth mine hand against him. So David stayed his servants, and suffered them not to rise against Saul. Saul rose and went on his way.

David went out of the cave and cried after Saul, saying, My lord the king, wherefore hearest thou men's words, saying, David seeketh thy hurt? This day thine eyes have seen how the Lord had delivered thee into mine hand, and some bade me kill thee: but mine eye spared thee; and I said, I will not put forth mine hand against my lord; for he is the Lord's anointed. Moreover, my father, see the skirt of thy robe in my hand: for in that I cut off the skirt of thy robe, and killed thee not, know thou that there is neither evil nor transgression in mine hand.

It came to pass, when David had made an end of speaking these words, that Saul said, Is this thy voice, my son David? And Saul lifted up his voice, and wept. He said to David, Thou art more righteous than I: for thou hast rewarded me good, whereas I have rewarded thee evil. And thou hast shewed this day how thou hast dealt well with me: for thou killedst me not. Now I know well that thou shalt surely be king, and that the kingdom of Israel shall be established in thine hand. Swear now by the Lord, that thou wilt not cut off my seed after me, and that thou wilt not destroy my name out of my father's house.

David sware unto Saul. Saul went home; but David and his men gat up unto the hold.

1 Samuel xxiv

SHEEP-COTE

An under-shepherd looked after the sheep at night for several shepherds. In the morning, each shepherd would collect his own flock.

The walls of the sheep-cote were covered with thorn-bushes. There was often a shelter built on one side of the pen.

When there was a danger from robbers, look-out towers were built.

> "*To cover his feet.*"
>   This was a way of saying,
> "He went to sleep."
> "*Gat up unto the hold.*"
>   This means, "They returned to their stronghold."

SHEEP

They belonged to the head of the family. He often had many thousands. From them he got wool, milk, meat, fat, leather, and horn.

*DEATH OF SAUL

The Philistines fought against Israel: and the men of Israel fled from before the Philistines, and fell down slain in mount Gilboa. The Philistines followed hard upon Saul and upon his sons; and slew Jonathan, and Abinadab, and Malchi-shua, Saul's sons.

And the battle went sore against Saul, and the archers hit him, and he was sore wounded of the archers. Then said Saul unto his armour-bearer, Draw thy sword, and thrust me through. But his armourbearer would not; for he was sore afraid. Therefore Saul took a sword, and fell upon it. And when his armourbearer saw that Saul was dead, he fell likewise upon his sword, and died with him.

And when the men of Israel saw that Saul and his sons were dead, they forsook the cities, and fled; and the Philistines came and dwelt in them.

And it came to pass on the morrow, when the Philistines came to strip the slain, that they found Saul and his three sons. And they cut off his head, and stripped off his armour. And they put his armour in the house of Ashtaroth: and they fastened his body to the wall of Beth-shan. And when the inhabitants of Jabesh-Gilead heard of that which the Philistines had done to Saul; all the valiant men arose, and went all night, and took the body of Saul and the bodies of his sons from the wall of Beth-shan, and came to Jabesh, and burnt them there. And they took their bones, and buried them under a tree at Jabesh, and fasted seven days.

1 Samuel xxxi

*NEWS BROUGHT TO DAVID

Now it came to pass after the death of Saul, when David was returned from the slaughter of the Amalekites, a man came out of the camp from Saul, and David said unto him, From whence comest thou? And he said, Out of the camp of Israel am I escaped. And David said unto him, How went the matter? I pray thee, tell me. And he answered, The people are fled from the battle, and many of the people also are dead; and Saul and Jonathan his son are dead also. And David said unto the young man, How knowest thou that Saul and Jonathan be dead? And the young man said, As I happened by chance upon mount Gilboa, Saul leaned upon his spear; and the chariots and horsemen followed hard after him. And when he saw me he called, Stand, I pray thee, upon me, and slay

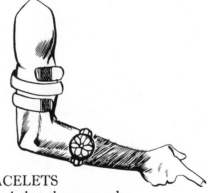

CROWN

No picture has been found of a Hebrew crown. It may have been a cap with a broad band of gold.

ASHTORETH

A Canaanite goddess of love. The Greeks called her Aphrodite, and the Romans Venus. Saul's armour was laid on her altar. As an insult, his body was hung on the walls of the city.

A LUCKY CHARM

This lucky charm, nearly 2000 years old, shows the goddess Ashtoreth.

BRACELETS

These showed that the men who wore them were kings or princes, because at that time the iron of which they were made was very valuable.

THE DEATH OF THE MESSENGER

The messenger brought Saul's crown and bracelets to David. He hoped for a reward, and told David that he had slain king Saul. David had him put to death, because he had killed the man chosen by God to be ruler of Israel.

---

me, because my life is yet whole in me. So I stood upon him, and slew him. And David said unto him, How wast thou not afraid to stretch forth thine hand to destroy the Lord's anointed? And David called one of the young men, and said, Fall upon him. And he smote him that he died. And David said, Thy mouth hath testified against thee, saying, I have slain the Lord's anointed.

And David lamented over Saul, and over Jonathan.

2 Samuel i

*DAVID THE KING—HIS KINDNESS

And Jonathan had a son that was lame. He was five years old when the tidings came of Saul and Jonathan out of Jezreel, and his nurse took him up, and fled: and it came to pass, as she made haste to flee, that he fell, and became lame. And his name was Mephibosheth.

And David said, Is there any that is left of the house of Saul, that I may shew him kindness for Jonathan's sake? And there was of the house of Saul a servant whose name was Ziba. And when they had called him unto David, the king said unto him, Is there not yet any of the house of Saul, that I may shew the kindness of God unto him? And Ziba said unto the king, Jonathan hath yet a son, which is lame on his feet. And the king said unto him, Where is he? And Ziba said unto the king, He is in the house of Machir, in Lo-debar. Then David sent, and fetched him from Lo-debar.

Now when Mephibosheth, the son of Jonathan, the son of Saul, was come unto David, he fell on his face, and did reverence. And David said unto him, Fear not: for I will surely shew thee kindness for thy father's sake, and will restore thee all the land of Saul thy father; and thou shalt eat bread at my table continually.

Then the king called to Ziba, and said unto him, I have given unto thy master's son all that pertained to Saul and to all his house. Thou, and thy sons, and thy servants, shall till the land for him, and thou shalt bring in the fruits, that thy master's son may have food to eat. Now Ziba had fifteen sons and twenty servants. Then said Ziba unto the king, According to all that my lord the king hath commanded his servant, so shall thy servant do. As for Mephibosheth, said the king, he shall eat at my table, as one of the king's sons.

So Mephibosheth dwelt in Jerusalem: for he did eat continually at the king's table: and was lame on both his feet.

2 Samuel iv.4; ix

*"THOU ART THE MAN"

David sent Joab, and his servants with him, and besieged Rabbah. David tarried at Jerusalem. And it came to pass in an eveningtide, that David arose from his bed and walked upon the roof of the king's house: and from the roof he saw a woman washing; the woman was very beautiful. David sent and inquired after the woman. And one said, Is not this Bath-sheba, the wife of Uriah the Hittite?

And it came to pass in the morning, that David wrote a letter to Joab, and sent it by the hand of Uriah. He wrote in the letter, Set ye Uriah in the forefront of the hottest battle, that he may be smitten, and die. It came to pass, when Joab observed the city, that he assigned Uriah unto a place where he knew that valiant men were. And there fell some of the people of the servants of David; and Uriah the Hittite died.

When the wife of Uriah heard that her husband was dead, she mourned for her husband. When the mourning was past, David fetched her to his house, and she became his wife, and bare him a son. But the thing that David had done displeased the Lord.

And the Lord sent Nathan unto David. He came unto him, and said, There were two men in one city; the one rich, and the other poor. The rich man had many flocks and herds: but the poor man had nothing, save one little ewe lamb. There came a traveller unto the rich man, and he spared to take of his own flock; but he took the poor man's lamb, and dressed it for the man that was come to him. David's anger was kindled against the man; and he said, As the Lord liveth, the man that hath done this thing shall surely die, and he shall restore the lamb fourfold. Nathan said to David, Thou art the man. Thus saith the Lord God of Israel, I anointed thee king over Israel, and I delivered thee out of the hand of Saul. Wherefore hast thou despised the commandment of the Lord, to do evil in his sight? thou hast killed Uriah the Hittite, and hast taken his wife to be thy wife. David said unto Nathan, I have sinned against the Lord. Nathan said unto David, Thou shalt not die. Howbeit, the child that is born to thee shall surely die.

Nathan departed unto his house. And the Lord struck the child that Uriah's wife bare unto David, and it was very sick. David therefore besought God for the child; and David fasted.

It came to pass on the seventh day that the child died. And the servants of David feared to tell him that the child was dead. But when David saw that his servants whispered, David perceived that the child was dead. Then David washed, and anointed himself, and changed his apparel, and came into the house of the Lord and worshipped: then he came to his own house; and when he required, they set bread before him and he did eat.

Then said his servants, Thou didst fast and weep for the child, while it was alive; but when the child was dead, thou didst rise and eat bread. And he said, While the child was yet alive, I fasted and wept: for I said, Who can tell whether God will be gracious to me, that the child may live? But now he is dead, can I bring him back again? I shall go to him, but he shall not return to me.

And David comforted Bath-sheba his wife: and she bare a son, and he called his name Solomon: and the Lord loved him.

2 Samuel xi.1-3, 14-17, 26-27; xii.1-10, 13-24

CLAY TABLET

In some Middle Eastern countries, writing was done on soft clay with a stylus.

Letters were sealed in an envelope of clay, which was then baked.

STYLUS

A wedge-shaped stick. The writing made with it is called *cuneiform* (*cuneus* = wedge).

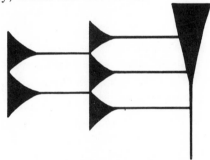

CUNEIFORM

The Sumerians invented writing about 6000 years ago. This was their word for "father".

◁ (b symbol)	b
◁	d
⩸	h
↓	k
⅔	m
⅘	n
⊃	p
†	t

EARLY WRITING

About 1000 B.C., the Israelites began to use ink, brush, and papyrus, instead of clay. They changed their writing to the shapes shown on the right. These shapes stood for sounds. They slowly changed to the shapes we use to-day.

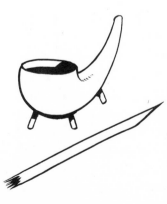

BRUSH AND INK HORN

Ink was made from soot mixed with gum arabic. It was kept in a horn.

The brush was a reed, frayed at the end.

*ABSALOM

And it came to pass that Absalom prepared chariots and horses, and fifty men to run before him. And Absalom rose early, and stood beside the way of the gate, and when any man that had a controversy came to the king for judgment, then Absalom called unto him, and said, Of what city art thou? And he said, Thy servant is of one of the tribes of Israel. And Absalom said unto him, See, thy matters are good and right; but there is no man deputed of the king to hear thee. Oh that I were made judge in the land, that every man which hath any suit or cause might come unto me, and I would do him justice! And it was so, that when any man came to him to do him obeisance, he put forth his hand, and took him, and kissed him. And on this manner Absalom stole the hearts of the men of Israel.

Absalom sent spies throughout all the tribes of Israel, saying, As soon as ye hear the sound of the trumpet, then ye shall say, Absalom reigneth in Hebron.

With Absalom went two hundred men out of Jerusalem. The conspiracy was strong; for the people increased continually with Absalom. David said unto his servants that were with him at Jerusalem, Arise, let us flee; for we shall not else escape from Absalom: make speed to depart, lest he overtake us suddenly, and smite the city with the edge of the sword.

And David sent forth a third of the people under Joab, a third under Abishai, and a third under Ittai. And the king stood by the gate side, and the people came out by hundreds and by thousands. The king commanded Joab, Abishai, and Ittai, saying, Deal gently with the young man Absalom.

ABSALOM (*Contd.*)

So the people went out against Israel: and the battle was in the wood of Ephraim; and there was a great slaughter that day of twenty thousand men. And Absalom met the servants of David. Absalom rode upon a mule, and the mule went under the thick boughs of a great oak, and his head caught hold of the oak, and he was taken up between heaven and earth; and the mule that was under him went away. A certain man saw it, and told Joab, and said, I saw Absalom hanged in an oak. Joab said unto the man, Why didst thou not smite him to the ground? I would have given thee ten shekels of silver, and a girdle. The man said unto Joab, Though I should receive a thousand shekels of silver, yet would I not put forth mine hand against the king's son: for in our hearing the king charged thee saying, Beware that none touch the young man Absalom. Then said Joab, I may not tarry thus with thee. He took three darts in his hand, and thrust them through the heart of Absalom. And ten men that bare Joab's armour smote Absalom and slew him. Joab blew the trumpet and the people returned from pursuing after Israel. And they took Absalom, and cast him into a great pit in the wood.

Then said Joab to Cushi, Go tell the king what thou hast seen. Then said Ahimaaz, Let me, I pray thee, also run. Then Ahimaaz ran by the way of the plain, and overran Cushi.

David sat between the two gates: and the watchman went to the roof over the gate, and lifted up his eyes, and looked, and behold a man running alone. And the king said, He cometh with good tidings. And Ahimaaz called, and said unto the king, All is well. And he fell upon his face before the king, and said, Blessed be the Lord thy God, which hath delivered up the man that lifted their hand against my lord the king. The king said, Is Absalom safe? Ahimaaz answered, I saw a great tumult but I know not what it was. The king said unto him, Turn aside, and stand here.

And Cushi came; and Cushi said, Tidings, my lord the king: for the Lord hath avenged thee this day of all them that rose against thee. The king said unto Cushi, Is Absalom safe? Cushi answered, The enemies of my lord the king, and all that rise against thee, be as that young man is.

The king was much moved and went up to the chamber over the gate, and wept: and as he went he said, O my son Absalom, my son, my son Absalom! would God I had died for thee, O Absalom, my son, my son!

2 Samuel xv.1-6, 10-14; xviii

73

*SOLOMON CHOSEN TO BE KING

Now king David was old and stricken in years.

Then king David said, Call me Bath-sheba. She came into the king's presence, and stood before the king. And the king sware, and said, As the Lord liveth, that hath redeemed my soul out of all distress, even as I sware unto thee by the Lord God of Israel, saying, Assuredly Solomon thy son shall reign after me, and he shall sit upon my throne in my stead; even so will I certainly do this day.

Bath-sheba bowed her face to the earth, and said, Let my lord king David live for ever.

King David said, Call me Zadok the priest, Nathan the prophet, and Benaiah. And they came before the king. The king said unto them, Take with you the servants, and cause Solomon my son to ride upon mine own mule, and bring him down to Gihon. Let Zadok the priest and Nathan the prophet anoint him there king over Israel: and blow ye with the trumpet, and say, God save king Solomon. For he shall be king in my stead: and I have appointed him to be ruler over Israel and Judah. Benaiah answered the king, and said, Amen: the Lord God of my lord the king say so too. As the Lord hath been with my lord the king, even so be he with Solomon, and make his throne greater than the throne of my lord king David.

So Zadok the priest, and Nathan the prophet, and Benaiah, went down, and caused Solomon to ride upon king David's mule, and brought him to Gihon. Zadok the priest took an horn of oil out of the tabernacle, and anointed Solomon. They blew the trumpet; and all the people said, God save king Solomon. And all the people came after him, and the people piped with pipes, and rejoiced with great joy, so that the earth rent with the sound of them.

Now the days of David drew nigh that he should die; and he charged Solomon his son, saying, I go the way of all the earth: be thou strong therefore, and shew thyself a man; and keep the charge of the Lord thy God, to walk in his ways, to keep his statutes, and his commandments, and his judgments and his testimonies, as it is written in the law of Moses, that thou mayest prosper in all that thou doest, and whithersoever thou turnest thyself: that the Lord may continue his word which he spake concerning me, saying, If thy children take heed to their way, to walk before me in truth with all their heart and with all their soul, there shall not fail thee a man on the throne of Israel.

So David slept with his fathers, and was buried in the city of David.

1 Kings i.1, 28-40; ii.1-4, 10

THE TOWER OF DAVID AT JERUSALEM

Jerusalem was captured by David, and became his capital. It was known as the City of David. He built strong walls around it, and brought the Ark of the Lord into it. He made plans for a temple. In the years that followed, Jerusalem was destroyed many times. The tower shown above was built by Herod the Great, the king who tried to kill the baby Jesus.

THE SHIELD OF DAVID

Sometimes called Solomon's Shield, or the Shield of Abraham. It is a symbol used by Jews throughout the world.

It was a common design in Old Testament times, but was not used as a symbol until the Middle Ages, when Jews were forced to wear it on their backs as a sign of their religion.

In Nazi Germany, which subjected the Jews to terrible persecutions, they were once again forced to wear this badge, so that everybody might know to what race they belonged.

BUILDING THE TEMPLE

And Hiram king of Tyre sent his servants unto Solomon; for he had heard that they had anointed him king in the room of his father: for Hiram was ever a lover of David.

And Solomon sent to Hiram, saying, Thou knowest how David my father could not build an house unto the name of the Lord his God for the wars which were about him on every side. Now the Lord my God hath given me rest on every side, so that there is neither adversary nor evil occurrent. I purpose to build an house unto the name of the Lord my God, as the Lord spake unto David my father, saying, Thy son, whom I will set upon thy throne in thy room, he shall build an house unto my name. Now command thou that they hew me cedar trees out of Lebanon; and my servants shall be with thy servants: and unto thee will I give hire for thy servants according to all that thou shalt appoint: for thou knowest that there is not among us any that can skill to hew timber like unto the Sidonians.

And it came to pass, when Hiram heard the words of Solomon, that he rejoiced greatly, and said, Blessed be the Lord this day, which hath given unto David a wise son over this great people. And Hiram sent to Solomon, saying, I have considered the things which thou sentest to me for: and I will do all thy desire concerning timber of cedar and timber of fir. My servants shall bring them down from Lebanon unto the sea: and I will convey them by sea in floats unto the place that thou shalt appoint, and thou shalt accomplish my desire, in giving food for my household.

So Hiram gave Solomon cedar trees and fir trees according to his desire. And Solomon gave Hiram twenty thousand measures of wheat, and twenty measures of pure oil year by year. And there was peace between Hiram and Solomon.

And king Solomon raised a levy out of all Israel; and the levy was thirty thousand men. And he sent them to Lebanon, ten thousand a month by courses: a month they were in Lebanon, and two months at home. And Solomon had three score and ten thousand that bare burdens, and fourscore thousand hewers in the mountains.

And the king commanded, and they brought great stones, costly stones, and hewed stones, to lay the foundation of the house. And Solomon's builders and Hiram's builders did hew them, and the stonesquarers: so they prepared timber and stones to build the house.

1 Kings v; vi.7

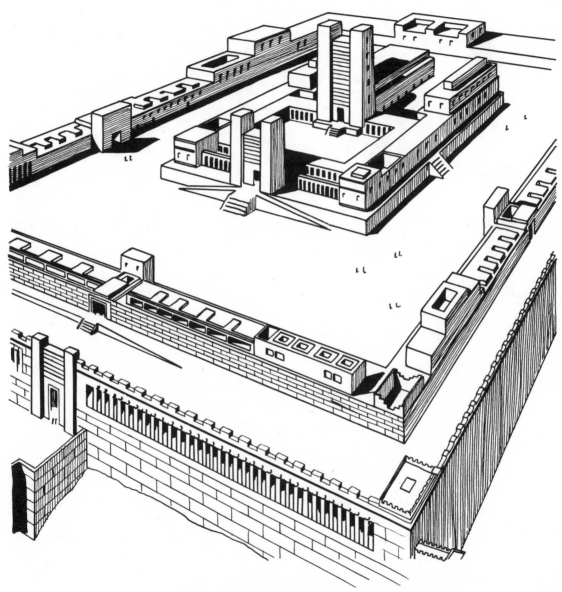

KING SOLOMON'S TEMPLE

The temple was built of white limestone, by Phœnician craftsmen led by an architect named Hiram. It was not very big, being only about 100 feet long, 60 feet wide, and 45 feet high. Only the priests and the king were allowed to enter it.

It took seven years to build, and was destroyed in the year 587 B.C., by the army of Nebuchadnezzar.

JACHIN AND BOAZ

Two copper pillars. They stood by the steps of Solomon's temple. Their names meant, "God had strength", and "God was strong".

CEDAR TREES

Solomon bought these trees from Hiram, king of Tyre. He used them to build his palace, the temple, and his ships.

A PHŒNICIAN MERCHANT SHIP

Solomon learned from the Phœnicians how to build ships. His ships sailed to Ophir (East Africa), and brought back gold, silver, and precious stones.

IRON

The Philistines kept the smelting of iron a great secret. When David defeated them he learned this secret. The Israelites then built great foundries for the smelting of copper and iron.

*ELIJAH FED BY THE RAVENS

Elijah said unto Ahab, As the Lord God of Israel liveth, there shall not be dew nor rain these years, but according to my word. And the word of the Lord came to him, saying, Turn thee eastward, and hide thyself by the brook Cherith. Thou shalt drink of the brook; and I have commanded the ravens to feed thee there. He did according to the word of the Lord. The ravens brought him bread and flesh, and he drank of the brook. After a while the brook dried up, because there had been no rain in the land.

1 Kings xvii.1-7

*ELIJAH AND THE WIDOW'S CRUSE

And the word of the Lord came to him saying, Arise, get thee to Zarephath. I have commanded a widow woman there to sustain thee. So he arose and went to Zarephath. When he came to the gate of the city, the widow woman was there gathering sticks. He called to her, Fetch me a little water that I may drink, and bring me, I pray thee, a morsel of bread. She said, As the Lord thy God liveth, I have but an handful of meal and a little oil in a cruse. I am gathering sticks that I may go in and dress it for me and my son, that we may eat it and die. Elijah said unto her, Fear not; make me thereof a little cake first, and bring it unto me, and after make for thee and thy son. For thus saith the Lord God of Israel, The barrel of meal shall not waste, neither shall the cruse of oil fail, until the day that the Lord sendeth rain. She went and did according to the saying of Elijah: and she and he, and her house, did eat many days.

1 Kings xvii.8-15

*ELIJAH—HEALING THE WOMAN'S SON

And it came to pass that the son of the woman fell sick; and there was no breath in him. She said unto Elijah, O thou man of God, art thou come to slay my son? And he said, Give me thy son. He took him and carried him up into a loft, and laid him upon his own bed. And he cried unto the Lord, O Lord my God, hast thou brought evil upon the widow with whom I sojourn, by slaying her son? And he stretched himself upon the child three times and cried, O Lord my God, I pray thee, let this child's soul come into him again. The Lord heard the voice of Elijah; and the soul of the child came into him again, and he revived.

The woman said to Elijah, Now by this I know thou art a man of God.

1 Kings xvii.17-24

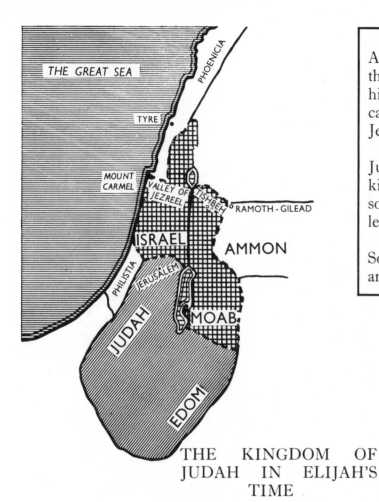

THE KINGDOM OF JUDAH IN ELIJAH'S TIME

THE TWO KINGDOMS

After the death of king Solomon, the people in the northern part of his kingdom revolted. They became the kingdom of Israel, under Jeroboam I.

The southern part, the tribes of Judah and Benjamin, became the kingdom of Judah, with Solomon's son Rehoboam as king. Jerusalem was the capital.

Fifty years after the death of Solomon, Ahab was king of Israel, and Jehoshophat king of Judah.

A STATUETTE OF BAAL

Ahab married Jezebel, daughter of the king of Tyre, who worshipped Baal and Astarte. The Lord was angry, and through Elijah punished the people of Israel.

ELIJAH BRINGING THE BOY TO LIFE.

*ELIJAH AND THE PROPHETS OF BAAL

It came to pass that the word of the Lord came to Elijah in the third year, saying, Go, shew thyself unto Ahab; and I will send rain upon the earth. Elijah went to shew himself. And Ahab called Obadiah, which was the governor of his house, and said, Obadiah, Go into the land, unto all fountains, and all brooks: we may find grass to save the horses and mules. So they divided the land between them to pass throughout it: Ahab went one way, and Obadiah went another way. And as Obadiah was in the way, Elijah met him: and he knew him, and fell on his face, and said, Art thou my lord Elijah? And he answered, I am: go, tell thy lord, Elijah is here. As the Lord of hosts liveth, before whom I stand, I will surely shew myself unto him this day. So Obadiah went to meet Ahab, and told him: and Ahab went to meet Elijah.

When Ahab saw Elijah Ahab said, Art thou he that troubleth Israel? And he answered, I have not troubled Israel; but thou, and thy father's house, in that ye have forsaken the commandments of the Lord, and thou hast followed Baalim. Now therefore send, and gather to me all Israel unto mount Carmel, and the prophets of Baal four hundred and fifty, and the prophets of the groves four hundred, which eat at Jezebel's table. And Elijah came unto the people and said, How long halt ye between two opinions? If the Lord be God, follow him: but if Baal, then follow him. The people answered not a word.

Then said Elijah, I, even I only, remain a prophet of the Lord; but Baal's prophets are four hundred and fifty men. Let them therefore give us two bullocks; and let them choose one for themselves, and cut it in

THE ALTAR OF ELIJAH

At the contest, Elijah built an altar of twelve stones. Each stone stood for one of the tribes of Israel.

ELIJAH

Elijah had long black hair, which was a sign of strength (see the story of Samson). He wore a girdle of skin, and a mantle or cape of sheepskin or camel-hair. The cape was a sign of mourning for the sins of the people.

DRESSING A BULLOCK

Offerings to God were part of the Hebrew way of worship. A bullock was offered to God, to show that the Israelites were sorry for their sins. Before the sacrifice, the bullock was made ready (*dressed*); by being killed and skinned.

pieces, and lay it on wood, and put no fire under. And call ye on the name of your gods, and I will call on the name of the Lord: and the God that answereth by fire, let him be God. The people answered, It is well spoken.

Elijah said unto the prophets of Baal, Choose one bullock for yourselves and dress it; for ye are many; and call on the name of your gods, but put no fire under. And they took the bullock and they dressed it, and called on the name of Baal from morning until noon. But there was no voice nor any that answered. At noon Elijah mocked them and said, Cry aloud, for he is a god: either he is talking, or he is pursuing, or he is in a journey, or sleepeth and must be awaked. And it came to pass, when midday was past, and they prophesied until the time of the offering of the evening sacrifice, that there was neither voice, nor any to answer.

Elijah said unto all the people, Come near unto me. And Elijah took twelve stones, and with the stones he built an altar in the name of the Lord: and he made a trench about the altar. He put the wood in order, and cut the bullock in pieces and laid him on the wood, and said, Fill four barrels with water, and pour it on the burnt sacrifice, and on the wood. And he said, Do it the second time. Do it the third time. They did it and the water ran round about the altar; and filled the trench. And Elijah came near and said, Lord God of Abraham, Isaac and of Israel, let it be known this day that thou art God in Israel, and that I am thy servant, and that I have done all these things at thy word.

Then the fire of the Lord fell, and consumed the burnt sacrifice, the wood, and the stones, and licked up the water that was in the trench. When all the people saw it they fell on their faces and said, The Lord, he is the God; the Lord, he is the God. And Elijah said unto them, Take the prophets of Baal; let not one of them escape.

1 Kings xviii.1-40

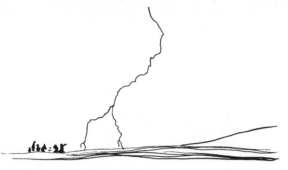

THE FIRE OF THE LORD
Lightning from a cloudless sky amazed the people. It proved that Elijah was speaking for God.

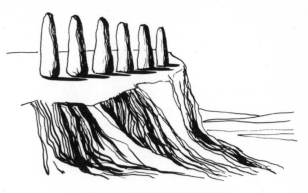

HIGH PLACES
The groves were set on high places. These had been places of worship from earliest times.

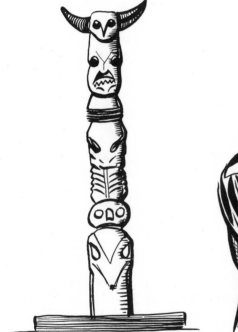

PROPHETS OF THE GROVES
The groves were not clumps of trees. They were poles or pillars of stones, set up for a heathen god. North American Indians used to do the same thing. Their poles were of wood.

JUDGMENT BY ELIJAH
Elijah condemned the prophets to death, because they had led the people away from the true God. This was the punishment laid down in Deuteronomy xiii.5.

*ELIJAH UNDER THE JUNIPER TREE

Ahab told Jezebel all that Elijah had done, and how he had slain all the prophets. Then Jezebel sent a messenger unto Elijah saying, So let the gods do to me, if I make not thy life as the life of one of them by to morrow about this time.

When he saw that, he arose, and went for his life, and came to Beersheba, and left his servant there. But he went a day's journey into the wilderness, and sat under a juniper tree: and he requested that he might die. As he lay and slept under a juniper tree an angel touched him and said, Arise and eat. And he looked, and behold, there was a cake baken on the coals, and a cruse of water at his head. And the angel of the Lord came the second time and said, Arise and eat, because the journey is too great for thee. He did eat and drink and went in the strength of that meat forty days and forty nights unto Horeb the mount of God.

1 Kings xix. 1-8

*ELIJAH AND THE STILL SMALL VOICE

And he came unto a cave and lodged there: and the word of the Lord came to him, and said, Go forth and stand upon the mount before the Lord. A great and strong wind rent the mountains and brake in pieces the rocks; but the Lord was not in the wind: and after the wind an earthquake: but the Lord was not in the earthquake, and after the earthquake a fire; but the Lord was not in the fire: and after the fire a still small voice. When Elijah heard it, he wrapped his face in his mantle, and went out and stood. There came a voice unto him, What doest thou here, Elijah? He said, I have been very jealous for the Lord God of hosts: because the children of Israel have forsaken thy covenant, thrown down thine altars, and slain thy prophets. I only am left and they seek my life:

The Lord said, Go, return on thy way to the wilderness of Damascus: and when thou comest anoint Hazael to be king over Syria, Jehu to be king over Israel: and Elisha shalt thou anoint to be prophet in thy room. It shall come to pass, that him that escapeth the sword of Hazael shall Jehu slay: and him that escapeth from Jehu shall Elisha slay. Yet I have left me seven thousand in Israel which have not bowed unto Baal.

1 Kings xix. 9-18

*THE MANTLE OF ELIJAH

He departed and found Elisha who
was plowing with twelve yoke of
oxen: and Elijah cast his mantle upon
him. He left the oxen and ran after
Elijah and said, Let me, I pray thee,
follow thee. He took a yoke of oxen,
and slew them, and boiled their flesh
with the instruments of the oxen,
and gave unto the people and they
did eat. Then he arose and went
after Elijah and ministered unto him.

1 Kings xix. 19-21

JUNIPER TREE

The juniper was probably a big bush called broom. It has few leaves and pinkish-white flowers. Its big root is made into charcoal.

CRUSE AND CAKES

The *cruse* was an earthenware jar. The cake was like a thick pancake, and was made of flour, water, and olive-oil.

"INSTRUMENTS OF THE OXEN"

These were the wooden yokes. Elisha used them to light a fire, on which he cooked the flesh of the oxen.

A YOKE

A *yoke* was a crossbar with two ropes. It joined two oxen. A "yoke of oxen" is a pair. Elisha must have been a rich man to have ploughed with twenty-four oxen. He gave up all his riches to be a prophet.

THE MANTLE OF ELIJAH

The cloak was a sign of a prophet. When Elijah gave Elisha his cloak, it was to show that Elisha was to be a prophet.

*SENNACHERIB

It came to pass in the fourteenth year of king Hezekiah, that Sennacherib king of Assyria came up against all the defenced cities of Judah, and took them, and sent Rabshakeh to Jerusalem unto king Hezekiah with a great army. Then came forth unto him Eliakim, which was over the house, Shebna the scribe, and Joah the recorder.

Rabshakeh said unto them, Say ye to Hezekiah, Thus saith the king of Assyria, On whom dost thou trust that thou rebellest against me? Lo, thou trustest in the staff of this broken reed, on Egypt; whereon if a man lean, it will go into his hand, and pierce it: so is Pharaoh king of Egypt to all that trust in him. But if thou say, We trust in the Lord our God: is it not he, whose altars Hezekiah hath taken away? Now therefore give pledges, I pray thee, to my master, the king of Assyria.

Then said Eliakim, Shebna and Joah, Speak, I pray thee, unto thy servants in the Syrian language and speak not to us in the Jews' language.

Then Rabshakeh cried with a loud voice in the Jews' language, Hear ye the words of the great king, the king of Assyria. Let not Hezekiah deceive you: hearken not to Hezekiah. Make an agreement with me by a present and come out to me: and eat ye everyone of his vine, and everyone of his fig tree, and drink ye everyone of the waters of his own cistern; until I come and take you away to a land like your own land, a land of corn and wine, a land of bread and vineyards. Beware lest Hezekiah say, The Lord will deliver us. Hath any of the gods of the nations delivered his land out of the hand of the king of Assyria? But they held their peace and answered him not a word.

Then came Eliakim, Shebna and Joah to Hezekiah and told him the words of Rabshakeh.

It came to pass when King Hezekiah heard it that he sent Eliakim, Shebna and the elders of the priests unto Isaiah, the prophet. Isaiah said unto them, Thus shall ye say unto your master, Thus saith the Lord, Be not

POOL OF SILOAM

KIDRON VALLEY

SPRING OF GIHON

SILOAM TUNNEL AND THE SPRING OF GIHON

When Hezekiah knew that Sennacherib was going to attack Jerusalem, he ordered his men to dig a tunnel more than 500 yards long, so that the people would not have to leave the walls of the city to get water.

SENNACHERIB ON HIS THRONE

Sennacherib ruled the Assyrian empire, which covered most of the Middle East. His capital was at Nineveh.

SCRIBES KEEPING RECORDS

Assyrian soldiers brought their prisoners and victims to the scribes to be counted.

afraid of the words thou hast heard, wherewith the servants of the king of Assyria have blasphemed thee. I will send a blast upon him, and he shall hear a rumour, and return to his own land; and I will cause him to fall by the sword in his own land.

So Rabshakeh returned, and found the king of Assyria warring against Libnah. And he heard say concerning Tirhakah king of Ethiopia, He is come forth to make war with thee. And when he heard it he sent messengers to Hezekiah, saying, Let not thy God, in whom thou trustest, deceive thee, saying, Jerusalem shall not be given into the hand of the king of Assyria. Behold thou hast heard what the kings of Assyria have done to all lands by destroying them utterly; shalt thou be delivered?

Hezekiah received the letter and read it, and went up unto the house of the Lord, and spread it before the Lord. And Hezekiah prayed unto the Lord.

Then Isaiah sent unto Hezekiah, saying, Thus saith the Lord God of Israel concerning the king of Assyria. He shall not come into this city, nor shoot an arrow there, nor come before it with shields, nor cast a bank against it. I will defend this city for mine own sake, and for my servant David's sake.

Then the angel of the Lord went forth and smote in the camp of the Assyrians a hundred and four score and five thousand. So Sennacherib departed and dwelt at Nineveh. And it came to pass as he was worshipping in the house of Nisroch that his sons smote him with the sword.

Isaiah xxxvi and xxxvii

*JERUSALEM TAKEN

Nebuchadnezzar king of Babylon came, he, and all his host, against Jerusalem, and pitched against it; and they built forts against it round about. The city was besieged and the famine prevailed in the city, and there was no bread for the people of the land. The city was broken up and all the men of war fled by night.

And in the fifth month came Nebuzaradan, captain of the guard, a servant of the king of Babylon, unto Jerusalem: he burnt the house of the Lord, and the king's house, and all the houses of Jerusalem, and every great man's house burnt he with fire. And the army of the Chaldees, that were with the captain of the guard, brake down the walls of Jerusalem.

2 Kings xxv.1-4, 8-10

*THE CAPTIVITY

These are the words of the letter that Jeremiah the prophet sent from Jerusalem unto the elders which were carried away captives, and to the priests, and to the prophets, and to all the people whom Nebuchadnezzar had carried away captive from Jerusalem to Babylon.

Thus saith the Lord of hosts, the God of Israel, unto all that are carried away captives, whom I have caused to be carried away from Jerusalem unto Babylon. Build ye houses, and dwell in them; and plant gardens, and eat the fruit of them. Take ye wives and beget sons that ye may be increased there, and not diminished. Seek the peace of the city whither I caused you to be carried away captives, and pray unto the Lord for it. After seventy years be accomplished at Babylon I will visit you, and perform my good word toward you, in causing you to return to this place. And I will be found of you: I will turn away your captivity, and I will gather you from all the nations, and from all the places whither I have driven you; and I will bring you again into the place whence I caused you to be carried away captive.

Jeremiah xxix.1-14

THE GOLDEN IMAGE

Nebuchadnezzar the king made an image of gold, whose height was three score cubits, and the breadth thereof six cubits: he set it up in the plain of Dura, in the province of Babylon. Then Nebuchadnezzar the king sent to gather together the princes, the governors, and the captains, the judges, the treasurers, the councillors, the sheriffs, and all the rulers of the provinces, to come to the dedication of the image; and they stood before the image that Nebuchadnezzar had set up.

Then an herald cried aloud, To you it is commanded, O people, nations, and languages, that at what time ye hear the sound of the cornet, flute, harp, sackbut, psaltery, dulcimer and all kinds of musick, ye fall down and worship the golden image that Nebuchadnezzar the king hath set up: and whoso falleth not down and worshippeth shall the same hour be cast into the midst of a burning fiery furnace. Therefore at that time, when all the people heard the sound of the cornet, flute, harp, sackbut, psaltery, and all kinds of musick, all the people, the nations, and languages, fell down and worshipped the golden image that Nebuchadnezzar the king had set up.

At that time certain Chaldeans came near, and accused the Jews. They spake and said to the king, Nebuchadnezzar, O king, live for ever. Thou, O king, hast made a decree that every man that shall hear the sound of the cornet, flute, harp, sackbut, psaltery, and dulcimer, and all kinds of musick, shall fall down and worship the golden image: and whoso falleth not down and worshippeth,

SPOILS OF WAR

The victors took loot back to their homes. Here they are seen using an Israelite cart.

WAR CHARIOT
This was the "tank" of long ago.

ASSYRIAN WARRIORS
The slingers were the artillery of ancient days. They were very much feared.

that he should be cast into the midst of a burning fiery furnace. There are certain Jews whom thou hast set over the affairs of the province of Babylon, Shadrach, Meshach and Abed-nego; these men, O king, have not regarded thee: they serve not thy gods, nor worship the golden image which thou hast set up.

Then Nebuchadnezzar in his rage and fury commanded to bring Shadrach, Meshach and Abed-nego. Then they brought these men before the king. Nebuchadnezzar spake and said, Is it true, O Shadrach, Meshach and Abed-nego, do not ye serve my gods, nor worship the golden image which I have set up? Now if ye be ready that at what time ye hear the sound of the cornet, flute, harp, sackbut, psaltery, and dulcimer, and all kinds of musick, ye fall down and worship the image which I have made; well: but if ye worship not, ye shall be cast the same hour into the midst of a burning fiery furnace; and who is that God that shall deliver you out of my hands?

Shadrach, Meshach and Abed-nego, answered and said to the king, O Nebuchadnezzar, we are not careful to answer thee in this matter. If it be so, our God whom we serve is able to deliver us from the burning fiery furnace, and he will deliver us out of thine hand, O king. But if not, be it known unto thee, O king, that we will not serve thy gods, nor worship the golden image which thou hast set up.

Then was Nebuchadnezzar full of fury, and he commanded that they should heat the furnace seven times more than it was wont to be heated.

Daniel iii.1-19

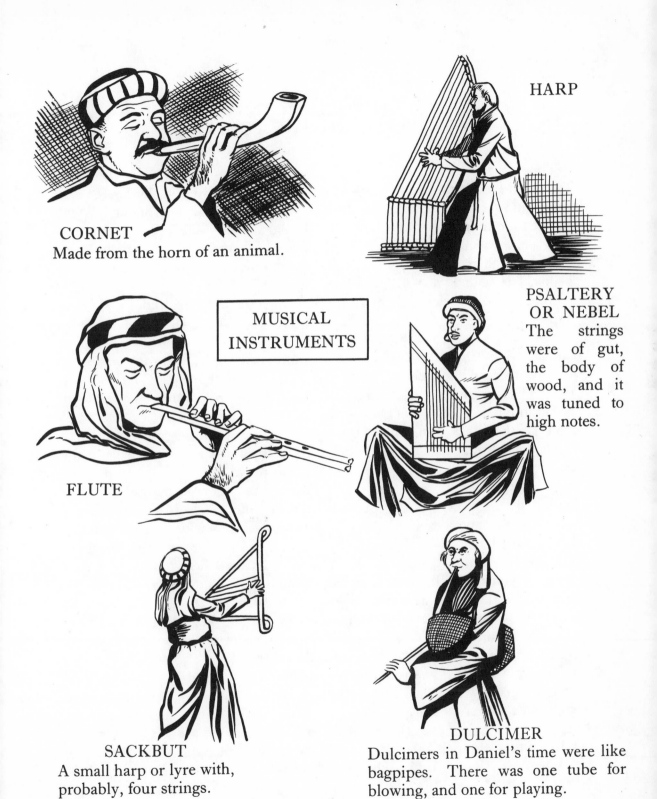

CORNET
Made from the horn of an animal.

HARP

PSALTERY
OR NEBEL
The strings
were of gut,
the body of
wood, and it
was tuned to
high notes.

MUSICAL
INSTRUMENTS

FLUTE

SACKBUT
A small harp or lyre with,
probably, four strings.

DULCIMER
Dulcimers in Daniel's time were like
bagpipes. There was one tube for
blowing, and one for playing.

*THE RETURN TO JERUSALEM—
REBUILDING THE TEMPLE

Thus saith Cyrus king of Persia, The Lord God hath given me all the kingdoms of the earth; and he hath charged me to build him an house at Jerusalem, which is in Judah.

Who is there among you of his people? His God be with him and let him go to Jerusalem and build the house of the Lord.

Then rose up the chief of the fathers of Judah and Benjamin and the priests, and the Levites, with all them whose spirit God had raised, to go up to build the house of the Lord. And all they that were about them strengthened their hands with vessels of silver, with gold, with goods, and with beasts, and with precious things, beside all that was willingly offered.

In the second year of Darius the king came the word of the Lord by Haggai the prophet, saying, Is it time for you to dwell in your ceiled houses, and this house lie waste? Now therefore saith the Lord of Hosts; Consider your ways. Ye have sown much, and bring in little; ye eat, but ye have not enough; ye drink, but ye are not filled with drink; ye clothe you, but there is none warm; and he that earneth wages earneth wages to put it into a bag with holes.

Thus saith the Lord; Consider your ways. Go up to the mountain, and bring wood and build the house; and I will take pleasure in it, and I will be glorified, saith the Lord. Ye looked for much and it came to little. Why? Because of mine house that is waste.

Then Zerubbabel, and Joshua, the high priest, with all the remnant of the people, obeyed the voice of the Lord their God. And they came and did work in the house of the Lord, their God. And when the builders laid the foundations of the temple of the Lord, they set the priests in their apparel with trumpets, and the Levites with cymbals, to praise the Lord. And they sang together giving thanks unto the Lord; because he is good, for his mercy endureth for ever.

. . . . And the elders of the Jews builded, and they prospered. And they builded, and finished it, according to the commandment of the God of Israel, and according to the commandment of Cyrus and Darius, and Artaxerxes king of Persia. And this house was finished in the sixth year of Darius the king. And the children of Israel, the priests, and the Levites, and the rest of the children of the captivity, kept the dedication of this house of God with joy.

Ezra i; Haggai i; Ezra iii and vi

NEBUCHAD-NEZZAR

This is a cameo portrait of king Nebuchadnezzar, who took the Jews into captivity.

CYRUS, KING OF PERSIA

A portrait sculpture of Cyrus, the king who allowed the Jews to return to Jerusalem.

How the kings of Babylon wrote their names:

NEBUCHADNEZZAR

BELSHAZZAR

CYRUS

ARTAXERXES

THE WALLS OF JERUSALEM

One of the most dreadful things that a prophet could say was that a city should be "a town without walls". Walls were the only way to keep enemies out.

Nehemiah found the walls of Jerusalem broken down. He asked the people to leave their fields and rebuild the walls.

*THE RETURN TO JERUSALEM—
REBUILDING THE WALLS OF THE CITY

The words of Nehemiah. And it came to pass, in the twentieth year of Artaxerxes the king, that I took up wine, and gave it unto the king. Now I had not been beforetime sad in his presence: Wherefore the king said unto me, Why is thy countenance sad, seeing thou art not sick? Then I said unto the king, Let the king live forever: why should not my countenance be sad, when the city, the place of my fathers lieth waste, and the gates thereof are consumed with fire?

Then the king said unto me, For what dost thou make request? I said unto the king, If it please the king, that thou wouldest send me unto Judah unto the city of my fathers that I may build it.

So it pleased the king to send me. Moreover I said unto the king, If it please the king, let letters be given me to the governors beyond the river, that they may convey me over till I come into Judah; and a letter unto Asaph the keeper of the king's forest, that he may give me timber for the gates of the palace, for the wall of the city, and for the house I shall enter into. And the king granted me. So I came to Jerusalem.

I was there three days and I arose in the night, I and some few men with me. And I went out by night and viewed the walls of Jerusalem, which were broken down, and the gates thereof consumed with fire.

Then said I unto the people, Ye see the distress that we are in, how Jerusalem lieth waste, and the gates thereof are burned with fire; come, let us build up the wall of Jerusalem, that we be no more a reproach. Then I told them of the hand of God which was upon me; also the king's words he had spoken to me. They said, Let us rise up and build.

. . . So we built the wall; for the people had a mind to work. But it came to pass, that when Sanballat, and Tobiah, and the Arabians, and the Ammonites, and the Ashdodites, heard that the walls of Jerusalem were made up, and the breaches began to be stopped, then they were very wroth, and conspired together to come and fight against Jerusalem. Nevertheless we made our prayer to God.

And I said unto the people, Be ye not afraid; remember the Lord, which is great and terrible, and fight for your brethren, your sons, your daughters, your wives and your houses. We returned every one unto his work.

From that time forth, half of my servants wrought in the work, and the other half held the spears, the shields, and the bows. For the builders, every one had his sword girded by his side.

So the wall was finished in fifty and two days. And it came to pass that all the heathen perceived that this work was wrought of our God.

Nehemiah i, ii, iv, vi

A SCROLL

The scrolls or scriptures were written on parchment and rolled on to two sticks. They were read by holding the right-hand stick, and rolling the scroll on to the left-hand stick. Scrolls of the early books of the Bible are very precious.

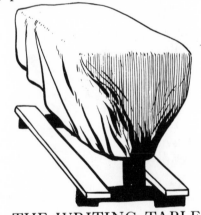

THE WRITING TABLE

At tables like this the scribes wrote the scrolls. They wrote on small sheets of parchment a little bigger than an exercise book. These were then sewn together to make a strip. A strip was usually about 24 feet long, but some rolls were as long as 144 feet.

SCROLL JAR

The scrolls were kept in clay jars for safety. In times of danger the jars were sealed and hidden in caves.

INK WELLS

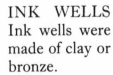

Ink wells were made of clay or bronze.

The ink was made of soot or gum.

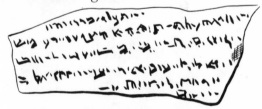

THE DEAD SEA SCROLLS

In 1947, in a cave near the Dead Sea, were found a number of very old scrolls. They are the oldest books of the Scriptures ever found. They were written about 200 years before Jesus was born.

They are so old that the parchment has crumbled or stuck together. In Jerusalem small pieces like this are being put together like a jigsaw puzzle.

The New Testament

THE BIRTH OF JESUS
AT BETHLEHEM

And it came to pass in those days, that there went out a decree from Cæsar Augustus, that all the world should be taxed. (And this taxing was first made when Cyrenius was governor of Syria.) And all went to be taxed, every one into his own city.

And Joseph also went up from Galilee, out of the city of Nazareth, into Judæa, unto the city of David, which is called Bethlehem; (because he was of the house and lineage of David:) to be taxed with Mary his espoused wife, being great with child.

And so it was, that, while they were there, the days were accomplished that she should be delivered. And she brought forth her firstborn son, and wrapped him in swaddling clothes, and laid him in a manger; because there was no room for them in the inn.

Luke ii.1-7

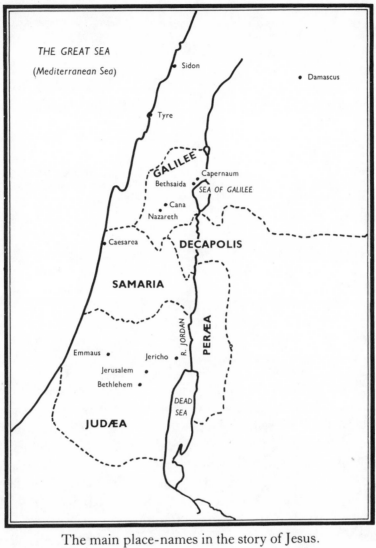

The main place-names in the story of Jesus.

The birthplace of Jesus may have been in a cave under or near the lodging house. No trace of stables, as we know them today, has been found and it is likely that the caves were made use of.

A Roman Governor. Cyrenius, Governor of Syria, ordered a census in order to have a check on the payment of taxes.

103

THE SHEPHERDS

And there were in the same country shepherds abiding in the field, keeping watch over their flock by night. And, lo, the angel of the Lord came upon them, and the glory of the Lord shone round about them: and they were sore afraid. And the angel said unto them, Fear not: for, behold, I bring you good tidings of great joy, which shall be to all people. For unto you is born this day in the city of David a Saviour, which is Christ the Lord. And this shall be a sign unto you; Ye shall find the babe wrapped in swaddling clothes, lying in a manger. And suddenly there was with the angel a multitude of the heavenly host praising God, and saying, Glory to God in the highest, and on earth peace, good will toward men.

And it came to pass, as the angels were gone away from them into heaven, the shepherds said one to another, Let us now go even unto Bethlehem, and see this thing which is come to pass, which the Lord hath made known unto us.

And they came with haste, and found Mary, and Joseph, and the babe lying in a manger. And when they had seen it, they made known abroad the saying which was told them concerning this child. And all they that heard it wondered at those things which were told them by the shepherds. But Mary kept all these things, and pondered them in her heart.

And the shepherds returned, glorifying and praising God for all the things that they had heard and seen, as it was told unto them.

Luke ii.8-20

Shepherds built mud-walled pens for their sheep. They slept across the only entrance so that the sheep could not get out and wild animals could not get in.

A bishop's crozier is the same shape as a shepherd's crook. It is a sign that he looks after people as the shepherd looks after sheep.

The Church of the Nativity. It stands on the spot where Jesus may have been born.

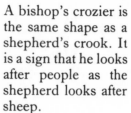

Young babies were wrapped in long lengths of cotton or linen cloth in the belief that their bones would grow straight.

A simple manger built of small stones and mortar, to hold the hay for animals.

THE WISE MEN

Now when Jesus was born in Bethlehem of Judæa, in the days of Herod the king, behold, there came wise men from the east to Jerusalem, saying, Where is he that is born King of the Jews? for we have seen his star in the east, and are come to worship him.

When Herod the king had heard these things, he was troubled, and all Jerusalem with him. And when he had gathered all the chief priests and scribes of the people together, he demanded of them where Christ should be born. And they said unto him, In Bethlehem of Judæa: for thus it is written by the prophet, And thou Bethlehem, in the land of Judah, art not the least among the princes of Judah: for out of thee shall come a Governor, that shall rule my people Israel.

Then Herod, when he had privily called the wise men, inquired of them diligently what time the star appeared. And he sent them to Bethlehem, and said, Go and search diligently for the young child; and when ye have found him, bring me word again, that I may come and worship him also.

When they had heard the king, they departed; and, lo, the star, which they saw in the east, went before them, till it came and stood over where the young child was. When they saw the star, they rejoiced with exceeding great joy.

And when they were come into the house, they saw the young child with Mary his mother, and fell down, and worshipped him: and when they had opened their treasures, they presented unto him gifts; gold, and frankincense, and myrrh.

And being warned of God in a dream that they should not return to Herod, they departed into their own country another way.

Matthew ii.1-12

A frankincense jar or flask
A milky-white gum with a sweet scent, from a tree grown in South Arabia. It was a symbol of holiness.

Myrrh
A sweet-smelling ointment used for embalming the dead. It was a symbol of suffering and death.

Jupiter and Saturn may have been close together in the sky at the time of the Wise Men and have looked like one star. Jupiter was thought to be a lucky and royal star and Saturn was supposed to protect Israel.

Gold
Always a valuable metal. It was a symbol of kingship.

Melchior, Gaspar and Balthazar are the names given by story-tellers to the Three Wise Men. One story says that one was white-skinned, one black and one yellow-skinned. Thus all races came to the birth of Jesus.

THE FLIGHT TO EGYPT, THE KILLING OF
THE BABES, AND THE RETURN TO NAZARETH

And, behold, the angel of the Lord appeareth to Joseph in a dream, saying, Arise, and take the young child and his mother, and flee into Egypt, and be thou there until I bring thee word: for Herod will seek the young child to destroy him.

When he arose, he took the young child and his mother by night, and departed into Egypt.

Then Herod, when he saw he was mocked of the wise men, was exceeding wroth, and sent forth, and slew all the children that were in Bethlehem, and in all the coasts thereof, from two years old and under, according to the time which he had diligently inquired of the wise men.

But when Herod was dead, behold, an angel of the Lord appeareth in a dream to Joseph in Egypt, saying, Arise, and take the young child and his mother, and go into the land of Israel: for they are dead which sought the young child's life.

And he arose, and took the young child and his mother, and came into the land of Israel. But when he heard that Archelaus did reign in Judæa in the room of his father Herod, he was afraid to go thither: notwithstanding, being warned of God in a dream, he turned aside into the parts of Galilee: and he came and dwelt in a city called Nazareth. And the child grew, and waxed strong in spirit, filled with wisdom: and the grace of God was upon him.

Matthew ii.13-23; Luke ii.40

In A.D. 533 a monk in Rome, Dionysius Exiguus, was asked to fix the date of Christ's birth. He made many errors and it is likely that the real date was seven years earlier.

CÆSAR AUGUSTUS

Herod the Great ruled for Cæsar Augustus. He was a harsh, cruel man who had thousands put to death. His son, Archelaus, was little better. He had 3000 Jews killed after he came to the throne. This was why Joseph was afraid to return to Judæa.

Near Cairo, in the grounds of the Church of the Holy Family, built by Jesuits, there is a fig tree with a charming story. Mary and Jesus are said to have hidden in the hollow trunk to escape the soldiers. A spider then spun its web so that they were safely hidden.

The kind of home into which Jesus was born.

1. Beds—These were rolled up when not in use.
2. Corn bin—Grain was stored in a bin and ground when it was needed, because flour did not keep very well.
3. Animals—These were kept on the lower floor.
4. Mats—These covered the bare earth floor.
5. Roof—Made of branches covered with mud or leaves.
6. Oil cruse—Palm or olive oil was precious and used for cooking.
7. Water jar—This was filled twice a day.
8. Walls—Made of straw and mud they were very thick to keep the heat out and warmth in.

JESUS IN THE TEMPLE

Now his parents went to Jerusalem every year at the feast of the passover. And when he was twelve years old, they went up to Jerusalem after the custom of the feast. And when they had fulfilled the days, as they returned, the child Jesus tarried behind in Jerusalem; and Joseph and his mother knew not of it. But they, supposing him to have been in the company, went a day's journey; and they sought him among their kinsfolk and acquaintance. And when they found him not, they turned back again to Jerusalem, seeking him.

And it came to pass, that after three days they found him in the temple, sitting in the midst of the doctors, both hearing them, and asking them questions. And all that heard him were astonished at his understanding and answers. And when they saw him, they were amazed: and his mother said unto him, Son, why hast thou thus dealt with us? behold, thy father and I have sought thee sorrowing. And he said unto them, How is it that ye sought me? wist ye not that I must be about my Father's business?

And they understood not the saying which he spake unto them. And he went down with them, and came to Nazareth, and was subject unto them: but his mother kept all these sayings in her heart.

And Jesus increased in wisdom and stature, and in favour with God and man.

Luke ii.41-52

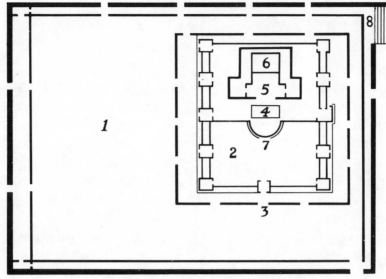

THE TEMPLE OF HEROD

Built by a thousand specially trained priests on the site of Solomon's temple. It took eighteen months to build. It was destroyed by the soldiers of Titus in A.D. 70. The building was 150 feet long and 105 feet wide.

1. Court of the Gentiles—Non-Jews were allowed here.
2. Women's court—Women could not join the men in worship.
3. Gates.
4. Altar—See drawing on this page.
5. Temple—Only men of Israel allowed here.
6. Holy of Holies—Where the ark was kept.
7. Upper Gate—Guarded day and night.
8. Steps to fortress of Antonia —The Roman guards could see into the court and stop any riots.

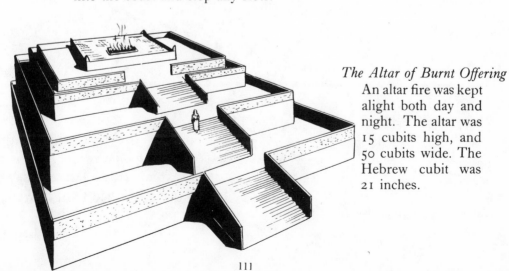

The Altar of Burnt Offering
An altar fire was kept alight both day and night. The altar was 15 cubits high, and 50 cubits wide. The Hebrew cubit was 21 inches.

111

THE PREACHING OF JOHN THE BAPTIST

In those days came John the Baptist, preaching in the wilderness of Judæa, and saying, Repent ye: for the kingdom of heaven is at hand. For this is he that was spoken of by the prophet Esaias, saying,
The voice of one crying in the wilderness,
Prepare ye the way of the Lord,
Make his paths straight.

And the same John had his raiment of camel's hair, and a leathern girdle about his loins; and his meat was locusts and wild honey.

Then went out to him Jerusalem, and all Judæa, and all the region round about Jordan, and were baptised of him in Jordan, confessing their sins.

But when he saw many of the Pharisees and Sadducees come to his baptism, he said unto them, O generation of vipers, who hath warned you to flee from the wrath to come? Bring forth therefore fruits meet for repentance: and think not to say within yourselves, we have Abraham to our father: for I say unto you, that God is able of these stones to raise up children unto Abraham.

And now also the axe is laid unto the root of the trees: therefore every tree which bringeth not forth good fruit is hewn down, and cast into the fire.

I indeed baptize you with water unto repentance: but he that cometh after me is mightier than I, whose shoes I am not worthy to bear: he shall baptize you with the Holy Ghost, and with fire: whose fan is in his hand, and he will throughly purge his floor, and gather his wheat into the garner; but he will burn up the chaff with unquenchable fire.

Matthew iii.1-12

THE BAPTISM OF JESUS

And it came to pass in those days, that Jesus came from Nazareth of Galilee, and was baptized of John in Jordan. And straightway coming up out of the water, he saw the heavens opened, and the Spirit like a dove descending upon him. And there came a voice from heaven, saying, Thou art my beloved Son, in whom I am well pleased.

Mark i.9-11

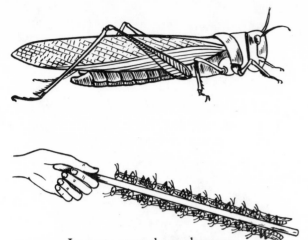

Locusts served on skewers

The locust is a kind of grasshopper. In Old and New Testament times they were the food of the poor. They were boiled in salty water and then dried in the sun. After the head, feet and wings had been taken away they were fried in butter and mixed with honey. They could also be smoked, boiled or roasted.

A swarm of locusts. When locusts swarm they fill the sky like a dark cloud. They strip the fields of every green thing wherever they land.

The dove. A symbol to the Jews of purity and harmlessness. It is now the symbol for peace.

"Raiment of camel's hair" was not a skin, but a coat of cloth woven from the hair of the camel. It is still worn today by the Arab bedouin.

BAPTISM

A sign of the washing away of sin so as to start a new life. It shows that the person is sorry for past wrongs and wants God to forgive him. John the Baptist was the first to baptize by complete bathing of the body instead of washing by hand, which had always been the custom.

THE FIRST DISCIPLES

Now as he walked by the sea of Galilee, he saw Simon and Andrew his brother casting a net into the sea: for they were fishers. And Jesus said unto them, Come ye after me, and I will make you to become fishers of men. And straightway they forsook their nets, and followed him. And when he had gone a little farther thence, he saw James the son of Zebedee, and John his brother, who also were in the ship mending their nets. And straightway he called them: and they left their father Zebedee in the ship with the hired servants, and went after him.

Mark i.16-20

SIMON'S MOTHER-IN-LAW

And forthwith, when they were come out of the synagogue, they entered into the house of Simon and Andrew, with James and John. But Simon's wife's mother lay sick of a fever, and anon they tell him of her. And he came and took her by the hand, and lifted her up; and immediately the fever left her, and she ministered unto them.

Mark i.29-31

Carp. The most common kind of fish in the Sea of Galilee.

Cat-fish. This could not be eaten by the stricter Jews. It was "unclean" because it did not have scales.

The fishermen on Lake Galilee used small single-sailed boats which held four to six men. During storms the sails were lowered and oars were used.

Sometimes the fishermen did not use boats but fished from the shore using a cast net called a shabakeh. As this net sank into the water it trapped the fishes, which could then be hauled ashore.

Much of the fish caught was cured by smoking it over a fire or rubbing salt into it.

LAKE GALILEE
The Lake of Galilee is often given other names and is sometimes called Lake Tiberius or Lake Gennesaret. It is about thirteen miles long, six miles wide and 700 feet below sea level.

THE PARALYTIC

And again he entered into Capernaum after some days; and it was noised that he was in the house. And straightway many were gathered together, insomuch that there was no room to receive them, no, not so much as about the door: and he preached the word unto them.

And they come unto him, bringing one sick of the palsy, which was borne of four. And when they could not come nigh unto him for the press, they uncovered the roof where he was: and when they had broken it up, they let down the bed wherein the sick of the palsy lay. When Jesus saw their faith, he said unto the sick of the palsy, Son, thy sins be forgiven thee. But there were certain of the scribes sitting there, and reasoning in their hearts, Why doth this man thus speak blasphemies? who can forgive sins but God only? And immediately when Jesus perceived in his spirit that they so reasoned within themselves, he said unto them, Why reason ye these things in your hearts? Whether is it easier to say to the sick of the palsy, Thy sins be forgiven thee; or to say, Arise, and take up thy bed, and walk? But that ye may know that the Son of man hath power on earth to forgive sins, (he saith to the sick of the palsy,) I say unto thee, Arise, and take up thy bed, and go thy way into thine house. And immediately he arose, took up the bed, and went forth before them all; insomuch that they were all amazed, and glorified God, saying, We never saw it on this fashion.

Mark ii.1-12

The roof was made of a mixture of mud and straw. It was easily broken and easily repaired.

Most houses had steps leading to a flat roof. The houses were built of sun-baked bricks and the flat roof was used as a store place, kitchen, or place for drying dates and figs.

In the hot season a tent was placed on the roof and the family would sleep there to escape the heat.

"SHOUTING FROM THE HOUSE TOPS"
It was the custom for merchants to climb the steps of houses near the market so that people could hear them more easily as they shouted out their wares.
The phrase "shouting from the house tops" has become part of our everyday language.

When the word "bed" is used in the Bible it means a kind of quilt which could be rolled up during the day and spread out for sleeping at night. Bedsteads were not used.

THE CALL TO MATTHEW

And as Jesus passed forth from thence, he saw a man, named Matthew, sitting at the receipt of custom: and he saith unto him, Follow me. And he arose, and followed him.

And it came to pass, as Jesus sat at meat in the house, behold, many publicans and sinners came and sat down with him and his disciples. And when the Pharisees saw it, they said unto his disciples, Why eateth your Master with publicans and sinners? But when Jesus heard that, he said unto them, They that be whole need not a physician, but they that are sick. But go ye and learn what that meaneth, I will have mercy, and not sacrifice: for I am not come to call the righteous, but sinners to repentance.

Matthew ix.9-13

These were the kind of coins which Matthew would have collected.

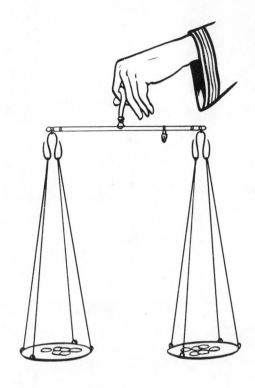

The tax collector would sometimes weigh coins to see if they had been clipped.

The receipt of custom was the place where dues or taxes were paid on people and goods that had crossed the Sea of Galilee. The tax collectors were sometimes called "Publicans". Matthew must often have collected taxes from the disciples who were fishermen.

The Gospels show that "publicans" were always classed with "sinners", a word of scorn and contempt.

TAX COLLECTORS

Tax collectors were Jews who had paid the Romans for the right to collect taxes for a year. They collected the taxes on the value of land, the harvest goods and produce for market. They were often able to make big profits by charging more than was just, and putting some of it in their own pockets.

The fact that they helped tax their own people to give money to the Romans made them the most hated section of the people.

119

THE BIRDS AND FLOWERS

Therefore I say unto you, Take no thought for your life, what ye shall eat, or what ye shall drink; nor yet for your body, what ye shall put on. Is not the life more than meat, and the body than raiment? Behold the fowls of the air: for they sow not, neither do they reap, nor gather into barns; yet your heavenly Father feedeth them. Are ye not much better than they? Which of you by taking thought can add one cubit unto his stature?

And why take ye thought for raiment? Consider the lilies of the field, how they grow; they toil not, neither do they spin: And yet I say unto you, That even Solomon in all his glory was not arrayed like one of these. Wherefore, if God so clothe the grass of the field, which to day is, and to morrow is cast into the oven, shall he not much more clothe you, O ye of little faith?

Therefore take no thought, saying, What shall we eat? or, What shall we drink? or, Wherewithal shall we be clothed? (For after all these things do the Gentiles seek:) for your heavenly Father knoweth that ye have need of all these things. But seek ye first the kingdom of God, and his righteousness; and all these things shall be added unto you. Take therefore no thought for the morrow: for the morrow shall take thought for the things of itself. Sufficient unto the day is the evil thereof.

Matthew vi.25-34

THE HOUSE BUILT ON A ROCK

Therefore whosoever heareth these sayings of mine, and doeth them, I will liken him unto a wise man, which built his house upon a rock: And the rain descended, and the floods came, and the winds blew, and beat upon that house; and it fell not: for it was founded upon a rock. And every one that heareth these sayings of mine, and doeth them not, shall be likened unto a foolish man, which built his house upon the sand: And the rain descended and the floods came, and the winds blew, and beat upon that house; and it fell: and great was the fall of it.

Matthew vii.24-27

THE LILY
A deep purple or scarlet flower, found all over the Middle East. The columns in Solomon's temple had carved lilies on them.

THE RED ANEMONE
This may have been the lily of which Jesus was speaking. It is very common in the valleys of Palestine.

THE OWL
A common bird. Some people believed that it was a ghost that carried off children.

THE SWALLOW AND SWIFT
Very common birds. They are the same as those seen in this country.

THE SOWER

There went out a sower to sow: And it came to pass, as he sowed, some fell by the way side, and the fowls of the air came and devoured it up. And some fell on stony ground, where it had not much earth; and immediately it sprang up, because it had no depth of earth: But when the sun was up, it was scorched; and because it had no root, it withered away. And some fell among thorns, and the thorns grew up, and choked it, and it yielded no fruit. And other fell on good ground, and did yield fruit that sprang up and increased; and brought forth, some thirty, and some sixty, and some an hundred. And he said unto them, He that hath ears to hear, let him hear.

And when he was alone, they that were about him with the twelve asked of him the parable. And he said unto them, Unto you it is given to know the mystery of the kingdom of God: but unto them that are without, all these things are done in parables: That seeing they may see, and not perceive; and hearing they may hear, and not understand; lest at any time they should be converted, and their sins should be forgiven them.

And he said unto them, Know ye not this parable? and how then will ye know all parables? The sower soweth the word. And these are they by the way side, where the word is sown; but when they have heard, Satan cometh immediately, and taketh away the word that was sown in their hearts.

And these are they likewise which are sown on stony ground; who, when they have heard the word, immediately receive it with gladness; And have no root in themselves, and so endure but for a time: afterward, when affliction or persecution ariseth for the word's sake, immediately they are offended.

And these are they which are sown among thorns; such as hear the word, and the cares of this world, and the deceitfulness of riches, and the lusts of other things entering in, choke the word, and it becometh unfruitful.

And these are they which are sown on good ground; such as hear the word, and receive it, and bring forth fruit, some thirtyfold, some sixty, and some an hundred.

Mark iv.3-20

PLOUGHING
This was done after the November rains, when the ground was soft.

SOWING
Wheat was sown in November, and barley in February.

THE FARMER'S YEAR

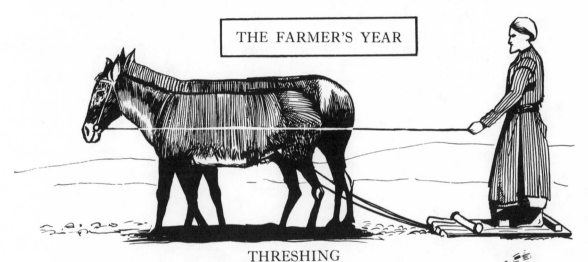

THRESHING
This was to separate the grain from the ears of wheat and to cut straw for fodder.

REAPING
Sometimes a sickle was used, but often the crop was pulled by hand.

WINNOWING
The threshed grain was tossed into the air. The heavy grain fell to the ground, and the light chaff and straw were blown away.

THE WEEDS IN THE CORN

Another parable put he forth unto them, saying, The kingdom of heaven is likened unto a man which sowed good seed in his field: But while men slept, his enemy came and sowed tares among the wheat, and went his way. But when the blade was sprung up, and brought forth fruit, then appeared the tares also. So the servants of the householder came and said unto him, Sir, didst not thou sow good seed in thy field? from whence then hath it tares? He said unto them, An enemy hath done this. The servants said unto him, Wilt thou then that we go and gather them up? But he said, Nay; lest while ye gather up the tares, ye root up also the wheat with them. Let both grow together until the harvest: and in the time of harvest I will say to the reapers, Gather ye together first the tares, and bind them in bundles to burn them: but gather the wheat into my barn.

Matthew xiii.24-30

THE MUSTARD SEED

Another parable put he forth unto them, saying, The kingdom of heaven is like to a grain of mustard seed, which a man took, and sowed in his field: Which indeed is the least of all seeds: but when it is grown, it is the greatest among herbs, and becometh a tree, so that the birds of the air come and lodge in the branches thereof.

Matthew xiii.31, 32

THE MUSTARD PLANT

A very common plant, with bright yellow flowers. Small birds are fond of its seed. It can grow as high as a man on horseback.

TARES

These were probably the bearded darnel, which looks like wheat until the grain is ripe. The roots of the bearded darnel entwine with those of the wheat, and the farmer cannot pull them up without damaging his crop.

Tare seed in bread causes sickness and dizziness.

BARLEY

One of the two main crops. It was the food of the poor. It was harvested about the middle of April in the plains, and at the beginning of May in the hill country.

WHEAT

This was harvested in the middle of May on the plains, and in July in the hill country. It was the main food, and a poor crop could be very serious.

THE MISSION

And he called unto him the twelve, and began to send them forth by two and two; and gave them power over unclean spirits; and commanded them that they should take nothing for their journey, save a staff only; no scrip, no bread, no money in their purse: but be shod with sandals; and not put on two coats. And he said unto them, In what place soever ye enter into an house, there abide till ye depart from that place. And whosoever shall not receive you, not hear you, when ye depart thence, shake off the dust under your feet for a testimony against them. Verily, I say unto you, It shall be more tolerable for Sodom and Gomorrha in the day of judgment, than for that city.

And they went out, and preached that men should repent. And they cast out many devils, and anointed with oil many that were sick, and healed them.

Mark vi.7-13

WALKING ON THE WATER

And straightway Jesus constrained his disciples to get into a ship, and to go before him unto the other side, while he sent the multitudes away. And when he had sent the multitudes away, he went up into a mountain apart to pray: and when the evening was come, he was there alone. But the ship was now in the midst of the sea, tossed with waves: for the wind was contrary.

And in the fourth watch of the night Jesus went unto them, walking on the sea. And when the disciples saw him walking on the sea, they were troubled, saying, It is a spirit; and they cried out for fear. But straightway Jesus spake unto them, saying, Be of good cheer; it is I; be not afraid.

And Peter answered him and said, Lord, if it be thou, bid me come unto thee on the water. And he said, Come. And when Peter was come down out of the ship, he walked on the water, to go to Jesus. But when he saw the wind boisterous, he was afraid; and beginning to sink, he cried, saying, Lord, save me. And immediately Jesus stretched forth his hand, and caught him, and said unto him, O thou of little faith, wherefore didst thou doubt? And when they were come into the ship, the wind ceased. Then they that were in the ship came and worshipped him, saying, Of a truth thou art the Son of God.

And when they were gone over, they came into the land of Gennesaret. And when the men of that place had knowledge of him, they sent out into all that country round about, and brought unto him all that were diseased; And besought him that they might only touch the hem of his garment: and as many as touched were made perfectly whole.

Matthew xiv.22-36

JESUS AND THE TWELVE

The disciples were the twelve chosen followers of Jesus. They lived with him, and learned his way of life. They were:

ANDREW: A fisherman and brother of Peter.

BARTHOLOMEW: A friend of Philip.

JAMES THE ELDER: A fisherman and brother of John. They were called the "Sons of Thunder".

JOHN: A fisherman, known as "The Beloved Disciple." He was a cousin of Jesus.

JAMES THE LESS (or YOUNGER): Son of Alphæus. Little is known about him.

JUDAS ISCARIOT: The only disciple who was not a Galilean. He looked after the money. He was not always honest.

JUDE: Little is known about him. He may have been a brother of Jesus.

MATTHEW: A tax collector. His name had been Levi.

PETER: Brother of Andrew and a fisherman. His real name was Simon, but Jesus called him *Cephas*, or *Peter*, which means "rock".

PHILIP: Little is known about him. He came from Bethsaida, from where Andrew and Peter also came.

SIMON: He was a *Zealot*, that is, a Jew who wanted to free his country from the Romans.

THOMAS: He was called *Didymus*, meaning "twin".

THE GOOD SAMARITAN

And, behold, a certain lawyer stood up, and tempted him, saying, Master, what shall I do to inherit eternal life? He said unto him, What is written in the law? how readest thou? And he answering said, Thou shalt love the Lord thy God with all thy heart, and with all thy soul, and with all thy strength, and with all thy mind; and thy neighbour as thyself. And he said unto him, Thou hast answered right: this do, and thou shalt live.

But he, willing to justify himself, said unto Jesus, And who is my neighbour? And Jesus answering said, A certain man went down from Jerusalem to Jericho, and fell among thieves, which stripped him of his raiment, and wounded him, and departed, leaving him half dead. And by chance there came down a certain priest that way: and when he saw him, he passed by on the other side.

And likewise a Levite, when he was at the place, came and looked on him, and passed by on the other side.

But a certain Samaritan, as he journeyed, came where he was: and when he saw him, he had compassion on him, and went to him, and bound up his wounds, pouring in oil and wine, and set him on his own beast, and brought him to an inn, and took care of him. And on the morrow when he departed, he took out two pence, and gave them to the host, and said unto him, Take care of him: and whatsoever thou spendest more, when I come again, I will repay thee.

Which now of these three, thinkest thou, was neighbour unto him that fell among the thieves? And he said, He that shewed mercy on him. Then said Jesus unto him, Go, and do thou likewise.

Luke x.25-37

THE GOOD SAMARITAN'S INN

This inn, on the road to Jericho, is supposed to be the inn to which the Good Samaritan took the wayfarer. Inns, in Biblical times and later, were not hotels, but shelters for travellers and their animals.

THE COURTYARD OF AN INN

In the large courtyard of an inn was a well. Around the sides were spaces for the travellers and their goods, and stalls for their animals. Travellers would bring their own food and fodder. At night they would spread a rug on the floor to sleep. Inns gave the traveller shelter from the cold and from robbers.

MARTHA AND MARY

Now it came to pass, as they went, that he entered into a certain village: and a certain woman named Martha received him into her house. And she had a sister called Mary, which also sat at Jesus' feet, and heard his word. But Martha was cumbered about much serving, and came to him, and said, Lord, dost thou not care that my sister hath left me to serve alone? bid her therefore that she help me. And Jesus answered and said unto her, Martha, Martha, thou art careful and troubled about many things: But one thing is needful: and Mary hath chosen that good part, which shall not be taken away from her.

Luke x.38-42

THE PHARISEE AND THE PUBLICAN

And he spake this parable unto certain which trusted in themselves that they were righteous, and despised others: Two men went up into the temple to pray; the one a Pharisee, and the other a publican. The Pharisee stood and prayed thus with himself, God, I thank thee, that I am not as other men are, extortioners, unjust, adulterers, or even as this publican. I fast twice in the week, I give tithes of all that I possess. And the publican, standing afar off, would not lift up so much as his eyes unto heaven, but smote upon his breast, saying, God be merciful to me a sinner. I tell you, this man went down to his house justified rather than the other: for every one that exalteth himself shall be abased; and he that humbleth himself shall be exalted.

Luke xviii.9-14

LEVITES
Dressed like the priests. Their job was to look after the Temple in Jerusalem and the synagogues in other big towns.

PRIESTS
Conducted the services, taught from the holy books, and led the prayers to God.

RABBI
A teacher, and a man greatly admired.

PHARISEES
People who obeyed the letter of the Law, but did not always have kind hearts to carry out good works.

SCRIBES
They copied and studied the Books of Law, and studied the Scriptures for the history of the people. They were lawyers and sometimes judges.

PUBLICANS
They bought from the Romans the right to collect taxes, and because of this were hated by everyone.

INVITATION TO A FEAST

And he put forth a parable to those which were bidden, when he marked how they chose out the chief rooms; saying unto them, When thou art bidden of any man to a wedding, sit not down in the highest room; lest a more honourable man than thou be bidden of him; And he that bade thee and him come and say to thee, Give this man place; and thou begin with shame to take the lowest room. But when thou art bidden, go and sit down in the lowest room; that when he that bade thee cometh, he may say unto thee, Friend, go up higher: then shalt thou have worship in the presence of them that sit at meat with thee. For whosoever exalteth himself shall be abased; and he that humbleth himself shall be exalted.

Then said he also to him that bade him, When thou makest a dinner or a supper, call not thy friends, nor thy brethren, neither thy kinsmen, nor thy rich neighbours; lest they also bid thee again, and a recompence be made thee. But when thou makest a feast, call the poor, the maimed, the lame, the blind: And thou shalt be blessed; for they cannot recompense thee: for thou shalt be recompensed at the resurrection of the just.

Luke xiv.7-14

PARABLE OF THE GREAT SUPPER

Then said he unto him, A certain man made a great supper, and bade many: And sent his servant at supper time to say to them that were bidden, Come; for all things are now ready. And they all with one consent began to make excuse. The first said unto him, I have bought a piece of ground, and I must needs go and see it: I pray thee have me excused. And another said, I have bought five yoke of oxen, and I go to prove them: I pray thee have me excused. And another said, I have married a wife, and therefore I cannot come. So that servant came, and shewed his lord these things. Then the master of the house being angry said to his servant, Go out quickly into the streets and lanes of the city, and bring in hither the poor, and the maimed, and the halt, and the blind. And the servant said, Lord, it is done as thou hast commanded, and yet there is room. And the lord said unto the servant, Go out into the highways and hedges, and compel them to come in, that my house may be filled. For I say unto you, That none of those men which were bidden shall taste of my supper.

Luke xiv.16-24

STOVE

A metal sheet placed over a fire of charcoal or dung. When the plate was hot the flat cakes of flour and oil were placed on it and cooked.

SPICE MILL

All food was flavoured with spices, which had to be ground to a fine powder. This was done in small wooden or stone hand-mills.

ARTICLES USED IN COOKING

FLOUR MILL

Flour was freshly ground for every meal. The mill was made of two stones. Grain was poured into the hole at the top. The top wheel was turned by the wooden handle and the flour collected from the side.

OIL JARS

In these clay jars the olive oil was kept. The necks were sealed with clay or wax.

PARABLE OF THE LOST SHEEP

And he spake this parable unto them, saying, What man of you, having an hundred sheep, if he lose one of them, doth not leave the ninety and nine in the wilderness, and go after that which is lost, until he find it? And when he hath found it, he layeth it on his shoulders, rejoicing. And when he cometh home, he calleth together his friends and neighbours, saying unto them, Rejoice with me; for I have found my sheep which was lost.

I say unto you, that likewise joy shall be in heaven over one sinner that repenteth, more than over ninety and nine just persons, which need no repentance.

Luke xv.3-7

PARABLE OF THE LOST SILVER

What woman having ten pieces of silver, if she lose one piece, doth not light a candle, and sweep the house, and seek diligently till she find it? And when she hath found it, she calleth her friends and her neighbours together, saying, Rejoice with me; for I have found the piece which I had lost. Likewise, I say unto you, there is joy in the presence of the angels of God over one sinner that repenteth.

Luke xv.8-10

LAMP

This was the kind of lamp used by the woman. It was made of earthenware, and was filled with olive oil. The wick was of cloth.

LAMP

This lamp was probably a temple lamp. On the top can be seen the seven-branched candlestick which was in the Temple at Jerusalem. The lamp shown was made in the fourth or fifth century A.D.

MONEY

The safest way to keep money was to wear it as jewellery. The piece of silver had probably fallen off the circlet on the woman's forehead. Circlets of coins were often given to a young woman as nowadays an engagement ring is given.

STORAGE JAR

Big jars like this, which stand about 30-36 inches high, were used to store oil or wine.

THE PARABLE OF THE PRODIGAL SON

A certain man had two sons. The younger of them said to his father, Father, give me the portion of goods that falleth to me. And he divided unto them his living.

Not many days after the younger son gathered all together, and took his journey into a far country, and there wasted his substance with riotous living. When he had spent all, there arose a mighty famine in that land; and he began to be in want. He went and joined himself to a citizen of that country; and he sent him into his fields to feed swine. And he would fain have filled his belly with the husks that the swine did eat: and no man gave unto him.

And when he came to himself, he said, How many hired servants of my father's have bread enough and to spare, and I perish with hunger! I will arise and go to my father, and will say, Father, I have sinned against heaven, and before thee, and am no more worthy to be called thy son: make me as one of thy hired servants.

He arose, and came to his father. When he was yet a great way off, his father saw him, ran, and fell on his neck and kissed him. The son said to him, Father, I have sinned against heaven, and in thy sight, and am no more worthy to be called thy son.

The father said to his servants, Bring forth the best robe, and put it on him; and put a ring on his hand, and shoes on his feet. Bring hither the fatted calf, and kill it; and let us eat, and be merry.

Now his elder son was in the field: and as he came and drew nigh to the house, he heard musick and dancing. He called one of the servants, and asked what these things meant. He said, Thy brother is come; and thy father hath killed the fatted calf, because he hath received him safe and sound.

And he was angry, and would not go in: therefore came his father out, and entreated him. He said to his father, Lo, these many years do I serve thee, neither transgressed I at any time thy commandment: yet thou never gavest me a kid, that I might make merry with my friends.

And he said unto him, Son, thou art ever with me, and all that I have is thine. It was meet that we should make merry, and be glad: for this thy brother was dead, and is alive again; and was lost, and is found.

Luke xv.11-32

HUSKS

These were the pods of the carob-tree. They were eaten by pigs, and also by the poor. They can sometimes be bought in sweet-shops, and are called locust- or honey-beans. When they are sent to other countries they are dried and pressed.

ROBE, RING, AND SHOES

When the father gave his son a robe, a ring, and shoes, it was to show that his son was no longer a servant.

The *robe* showed that the son was a *guest of honour*.

The *ring* showed that he had been given *authority*.

The *shoes* were a luxury, and showed that he was a *freeman*.

HIRED SERVANTS

They were poor relatives, who were paid for working in the house and fields.

PARABLES

The people whom Jesus was teaching were simple folk. He told them stories set in their everyday life. These they were able to understand.

Parables have been called "earthly sayings with heavenly meanings".

Thirty-one of the parables which Jesus told are in the Bible. Fifteen of them are about the kingdom of heaven, and sixteen are about how people should behave.

THE TRIUMPHAL ENTRY

And when they came nigh to Jerusalem, unto Bethphage and Bethany, at the mount of Olives, he sendeth forth two of his disciples, and saith unto them, Go your way into the village over against you: and as soon as ye be entered into it, ye shall find a colt tied, whereon never man sat; loose him, and bring him. And if any man say unto you, Why do ye this? say ye that the Lord hath need of him; and straightway he will send him hither.

And they went their way, and found the colt tied by the door without in a place where two ways met; and they loose him. And certain of them that stood there said unto them, What do ye, loosing the colt? And they said unto them even as Jesus had commanded: and they let them go. And they brought the colt to Jesus, and cast their garments on him; and he sat upon him. And many spread their garments in the way: and others cut down branches off the trees and strawed them in the way. And they that went before, and they that followed, cried, saying, Hosanna; Blessed is he that cometh in the name of the Lord: Blessed be the kingdom of our father David, that cometh in the name of the Lord: Hosanna in the highest.

And Jesus entered into Jerusalem, and into the temple: and when he had looked round about upon all things, and now the eventide was come, he went out unto Bethany with the twelve.

Mark xi.1-11

138

THE DIARY OF THE LAST WEEK

Day	Events		References
PALM SUNDAY	Jesus rode into Jerusalem. Spent the night at Bethany.		Mark xi.1-11 Matthew xxi.1-11, 14-17 . Luke xix.29-44 John xii.12-19
MONDAY	Turned the traders out of the temple. Spent the night at Bethany.		Matthew xxi.12-13 Luke xix.45-46
TUESDAY	In the temple. Stories of the Widow's Mite, the Talents, and the Foolish Virgins. Spent the night at Bethany.		Luke xxi.1-4
WEDNESDAY	The conspiracy. Spent the night at Bethany.		Matthew xxvi.1-16 Luke xxii.1-6 John xii.1-8
MAUNDY THURSDAY	The Last Supper. Peter's protest. Washing the disciples' feet. The arrest.		Matthew xxv.17-20 Luke xxii.7-30 Matthew xxvi.36-56 Luke xxii.39-53 John xviii.1-12
GOOD FRIDAY	Peter's denial. Trial before Pilate. The Crucifixion. The burial of Jesus.		Matthew xxvi.69-75 Mark xiv.66-72 John xviii.25-27 Matthew xxvii.1-61 Luke xxiii.1-56 John xix.1-42
SATURDAY	Jesus in the tomb.		Matthew xxvii.62-66

THE CLEANSING OF THE TEMPLE

And they came to Jerusalem: and Jesus went into the temple, and began to cast out them that sold and bought in the temple, and overthrew the tables of the moneychangers, and the seats of them that sold doves; and would not suffer that any man should carry any vessel through the temple.

And he taught, saying unto them, Is it not written, My house shall be called of all nations the house of prayer? but ye have made it a den of thieves. And the scribes and chief priests heard it, and sought how they might destroy him: for they feared him, because all the people was astonished at his doctrine.

And when even was come, he went out of the city.

Mark xi.15-19

THE WIDOW'S MITE

And Jesus sat over against the treasury, and beheld how the people cast money into the treasury: and many that were rich cast in much.

And there came a certain poor widow, and she threw in two mites, which make a farthing. And he called unto him his disciples, and saith unto them, Verily I say unto you, That this poor widow hath cast more in, than all they which have cast into the treasury: for all they did cast in of their abundance; but she of her want did cast in all that she had, even all her living.

Mark xii.41-44

TRADERS IN THE TEMPLE

Jews came from all over the known world to Jerusalem. They had to pay money when they went to the temple. Their money had to be changed into Jewish money. Money-changers made great profits. Animals had to be bought for sacrifice.

A MITE
(*Actual Size*)

The smallest copper coin. It was worth about a tenth of a penny in our money.

SILVER DENARIUS
(*Actual Size*)

This was a coin in everyday use. It was worth about sixteen cents in our money.

PALM TREE

This is a common tree in Palestine. Its fruit is the date.

THE FOOLISH VIRGINS

Then shall the kingdom of heaven be likened unto ten virgins, which took their lamps, and went forth to meet the bridegroom. And five of them were wise, and five were foolish.

They that were foolish took their lamps, and took no oil with them: but the wise took oil in their vessels with their lamps. While the bridegroom tarried they all slumbered and slept. And at midnight there was a cry made, Behold, the bridegroom cometh; go ye out to meet him. Then all those virgins arose, and trimmed their lamps.

And the foolish said unto the wise, Give us of your oil; for our lamps are gone out. But the wise answered, saying, Not so; lest there be not enough for us and you: but go ye rather to them that sell, and buy for yourselves.

And while they went to buy, the bridegroom came; and they that were ready went in with him to the marriage and the door was shut. Afterwards came also the other virgins, saying, Lord, Lord, open to us. But he answered and said, Verily I say unto you, I know you not. Watch therefore, for ye know neither the day nor the hour wherein the Son of man cometh.

Matthew xxv.1-13

(1) The bride is dressed by her bridesmaids.

A WEDDING

(2) The bridesmaids wait for the bridegroom.

(3) Meanwhile, the bridegroom has a party at his house.

(4) The bridegroom and his friends make their way to the bride's house.

(5) The bridesmaids wake, and go to meet the bridegroom.

(6) They all enter the house, and the doors are barred.

(7) The wedding feast begins.

*THE TALENTS

For the kingdom of heaven is as a man travelling into a far country, who called his own servants, and delivered unto them his goods.

And unto one he gave five talents, to another two, and to another one; to every man according to his several ability; and straightway took his journey.

After a long time the lord of those servants cometh, and reckoneth with them.

And so he that had received five talents came and brought other five talents, saying, Lord, thou deliveredst unto me five talents: behold, I have gained beside them five talents more. His lord said unto him, Well done, thou good and faithful servant: thou hast been faithful over a few things, I will make thee ruler over many things: enter thou into the joy of thy lord.

He also that had received two talents came and said, Lord, thou deliveredst unto me two talents: behold, I have gained two other talents beside them. His lord said unto him, Well done, good and faithful servant;

thou hast been faithful over a few things, I will make thee ruler over many things: enter thou into the joy of thy lord.

Then he which had received the one talent came and said, Lord, I knew thee that thou art an hard man, reaping where thou hast not sown, and gathering where thou hast not strawed: And I was afraid, and went and hid thy talent in the earth: lo, there thou hast that is thine. His lord answered and said unto him, Thou wicked and slothful servant, thou knewest that I reap where I sowed not, and gather where I have not strawed: Thou oughtest therefore to have put my money to the exchangers, and then at my coming I should have received mine own with usury. Take therefore the talent from him, and give it unto him which hath ten talents. For unto every one that hath shall be given, and he shall have abundance: but from him that hath not shall be taken away even that which he hath. And cast ye the unprofitable servant into outer darkness: there shall be weeping and gnashing of teeth.

Matthew xxv.14-30

THE TALENTS

There is an old story which tells us how the servants used the money.

THE SPICE-MERCHANT
The man with five talents. He bought spices in India, and brought them by ass-train and camel-train to Jerusalem.

THE FISH-MERCHANT
The man with two talents. He bought fish at Lake Galilee, salted it, and sold it in the markets at Jerusalem.

THE LAZY MAN
The man with one talent. He buried the silver in the ground, where it could do no good.

A TALENT
A talent was a weight of silver and not a coin. It was worth about **$** 1,000 in our money.

The story of the talents has given rise to our use of the word to mean "what you are able to do"; for example, when someone is told, "Do not waste your talents."

THE CONSPIRACY

After two days was the feast of the passover, and of unleavened bread: and the chief priests and the scribes sought how they might take him by craft, and put him to death. But they said, Not on the feast day, lest there be an uproar of the people.

And being in Bethany in the house of Simon the leper, as he sat at meat, there came a woman having an alabaster box of ointment of spikenard very precious; and she brake the box and poured it on his head. And there were some that had indignation within themselves, and said, Why was this waste of the ointment made? For it might have been sold for more than three hundred pence, and have been given to the poor. And they murmured against her. And Jesus said, Let her alone; why trouble ye her? she hath wrought a good work on me. For ye have the poor with you always, and whensoever ye will ye may do them good: but me ye have not always. She hath done what she could: she is come aforehand to anoint my body to the burying. Verily I say unto you, Wheresoever this gospel shall be preached throughout the whole world, this also that she hath done shall be spoken of for a memorial of her.

And Judas Iscariot, one of the twelve, went unto the chief priests, to betray him unto them. And when they heard it, they were glad, and promised to give him money. And he sought how he might conveniently betray him.

Mark xiv.1-11

146

SPIKENARD

A plant with a sweet scent. It grows in the mountains of India. It was very costly, because it had to be brought so great a distance.

OINTMENT

The custom of using ointment started in Egypt. Guests at a feast smeared scented ointment on their foreheads. As it melted, it cooled the face and gave off a pleasant smell.

Mary's ointment was worth the year's wages of a carpenter.

A HEBREW

This is a picture of a Jew at the time of Jesus. Jesus may have looked like this.

Jesus is sometimes called *Messiah*, which means "the anointed one". It comes from the Hebrew custom of marking a person for high office by anointing him.

THIRTY PIECES OF SILVER

Judas got thirty pieces of silver (the price of a slave) for betraying Jesus.

Judas kept the money-bag for the disciples. He used to help himself to what money he wanted. He wanted the ointment to be sold and the money to go into the money bag. He would then have been able to use some of it for himself.

He was annoyed when Jesus rebuked him, and this may have been why he sold Jesus to the priests.

THE LAST SUPPER

And the first day of unleavened bread, when they killed the passover, his disciples said unto him, Where wilt thou that we go and prepare that thou mayest eat the passover? And he sendeth forth two of his disciples, and saith unto them, Go ye into the city, and there shall meet you a man bearing a pitcher of water: follow him. And wheresoever he shall go in, say ye to the goodman of the house, The Master saith, Where is the guest-chamber, where I shall eat the passover with my disciples? And he will shew you a large upper room furnished and prepared: there make ready for us.

And his disciples went forth, and came into the city, and found as he had said unto them: and they made ready the passover. And in the evening he cometh with the twelve.

And as they sat and did eat, Jesus said, Verily I say unto you, One of you which eateth with me shall betray me. And they began to be sorrowful, and to say unto him one by one, Is it I? and another said, Is it I?

And he answered and said unto them, It is one of the twelve, that dippeth with me in the dish. The Son of man indeed goeth, as it is written of him: but woe to that man by whom the Son of man is betrayed!

good were it for that man if he had never been born.

And as they did eat, Jesus took bread, and blessed, and brake it, and gave to them, and said, Take, eat: this is my body. And he took the cup, and when he had given thanks, he gave it to them: and they all drank of it. And he said unto them, This is my blood of the new testament, which is shed for many. Verily I say unto you, I will drink no more of the fruit of the vine, until that day that I drink it new in the kingdom of God.

And when they had sung an hymn, they went out into the mount of Olives. And Jesus saith unto them, All ye shall be offended because of me this night: for it is written, I will smite the shepherd, and the sheep shall be scattered. But after that I am risen, I will go before you into Galilee. But Peter said unto him, Although all shall be offended, yet will not I. And Jesus saith unto him, Verily I say unto thee, That this day, even in this night, before the cock crow twice, thou shalt deny me thrice.

But he spake the more vehemently, If I should die with thee, I will not deny thee in any wise. Likewise also said they all.

Mark xiv.12-31

A CHALICE OR CUP

The cup used at the Last Supper has never been found. Many of the King Arthur stories tell how his knights tried to find this cup—the Holy Grail. There is a legend that Joseph of Arimathæa, a friend of Jesus, brought the Holy Grail to England and built a church at Glastonbury.

THE UPPER ROOM

It was in a room like this that Jesus and his disciples held the Last Supper.

THE LORD'S TABLE

The Last Supper is remembered in Christian churches all over the world. It is given many different names—Holy Communion, the Eucharist, Mass, the Breaking of Bread, the Thanksgiving, and the Lord's Supper.

WASHING THE DISCIPLES' FEET

Now before the feast of the passover, when Jesus knew that his hour was come that he should depart out of this world unto the Father, having loved his own which were in the world, he loved them unto the end.

And supper being ended, the devil having now put into the heart of Judas Iscariot, Simon's son, to betray him; Jesus knowing that the Father had given all things into his hands, and that he was come from God, and went to God; he riseth from supper, and laid aside his garments; and took a towel, and girded himself. After that he poureth water into a basin, and began to wash the disciples' feet, and to wipe them with the towel wherewith he was girded. Then cometh he to Simon Peter: and Peter saith unto him, Lord, dost thou wash my feet? Jesus answered and said unto him, What I do thou knowest not now; but thou shalt know hereafter. Peter saith unto him, Thou shalt never wash my feet. Jesus answered him, If I wash thee not, thou hast no part with me. Simon Peter saith unto him, Lord, not my feet only, but also my hands and my head. Jesus saith to him, He that is washed needeth not save to wash his feet, but is clean every whit: and ye are clean, but not all. For he knew who should betray him; therefore said he, Ye are not all clean. So after he had washed their feet, and had taken his garments, and was set down again, he said unto them, Know ye what I have done to you? Ye call me Master and Lord: and ye say well; for so I am. If I then, your Lord and Master, have washed your feet; ye also ought to wash one another's feet. For I have given you an example, that ye should do as I have done to you. Verily, verily, I say unto you, The servant is not greater than his lord; neither he that is sent greater than he that sent him. If ye know these things, happy are ye if ye do them.

John xiii.1-17

PETER'S PROTEST

And the Lord said, Simon, Simon, behold, Satan hath desired to have you, that he may sift you as wheat: but I have prayed for thee, that thy faith fail not: and when thou art converted, strengthen thy brethren.

And he said unto him, Lord, I am ready to go with thee, both into prison, and to death.

And he said, I tell thee, Peter, the cock shall not crow this day, before that thou shalt thrice deny that thou knowest me.

Luke xxii.31-34

WASHING OF FEET

When a visitor arrived, it was the custom for the host to tell a servant to wash the visitor's feet. This was done to remove the dust after walking through the hot countryside. It was a job usually done by the lowest servant.

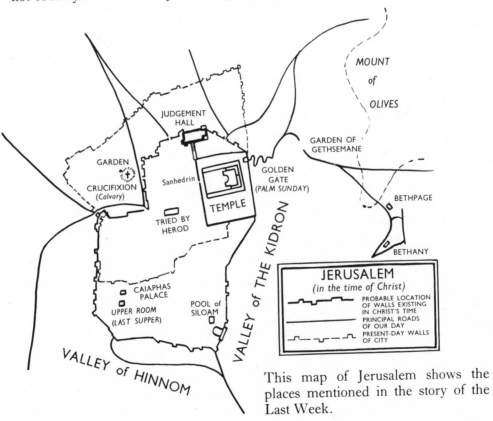

This map of Jerusalem shows the places mentioned in the story of the Last Week.

THE ARREST

And they came to a place which was named Gethsemane: and he saith to his disciples, Sit ye here, while I shall pray. And he taketh with him Peter and James and John, and began to be sore amazed, and to be very heavy; and saith unto them, My soul is exceeding sorrowful unto death: tarry ye here, and watch. And he went forward a little, and fell on the ground, and prayed that, if it were possible, the hour might pass from him. And he said, Abba, Father, all things are possible unto thee; take away this cup from me: nevertheless not what I will, but what thou wilt.

And he cometh, and findeth them sleeping, and saith unto Peter, Simon, sleepest thou? couldest not thou watch one hour? Watch ye and pray, lest ye enter into temptation. The spirit truly is ready, but the flesh is weak. And again he went away, and prayed, and spake the same words.

And when he returned, he found them asleep again, (for their eyes were heavy,) neither wist they what to answer him. And he cometh the third time, and saith unto them, Sleep on now, and take your rest: it is enough, the hour is come; behold, the Son of man is betrayed into the hands of sinners. Rise up, let us go; lo, he that betrayeth me is at hand.

And immediately, while he yet spake, cometh Judas, one of the twelve, and with him a great multitude with swords and staves, from the chief priests and the scribes and the elders. And he that betrayed him had given them a token, saying, Whomsoever I shall kiss, that same is he; take him, and lead him away safely. And as soon as he was come, he goeth straightway to him, and saith, Master, Master; and kissed him.

And they laid their hands on him, and took him. And one of them that stood by drew a sword, and smote a servant of the high priest, and cut off his ear. And Jesus answered and said unto them, Are ye come out, as against a thief, with swords and with staves to take me? I was daily with you in the temple teaching, and ye took me not: but the scriptures must be fulfilled. And they all forsook him, and fled.

And there followed him a certain young man, having a linen cloth cast about his naked body; and the young men laid hold on him: and he left the linen cloth, and fled from them naked.

Mark xiv.32-52

GETHSEMANE
A garden at the foot of the Mount of Olives, where there was an oil press from which it took its name.

POTTER'S FIELD
Judas, when he knew that Jesus was to be crucified, threw the money at the priests. With this money they bought land as a burial-place for strangers. It had been used by potters as a place from which they could take clay.

According to an old story, Judas tried to hang himself, but the rope broke and he was killed in the fall. He was the first person to be buried in the field.

THE SYMBOL OF MARK
Mark was once weak and timid, but, through his faith in God, became strong like a lion.

He may have been the young man in the linen cloth, who followed Jesus after the arrest.

He wrote the Second Gospel about A.D. 70.

THE KISS OF JUDAS
A kiss was the usual way of greeting a Rabbi. It was given on the cheek.

The words "kiss of Judas" are nowadays used when a person acts in a friendly way but all the time means to do harm.

PETER'S DENIAL

Then they took him, and led him, and brought him into the high priest's house. And Peter followed afar off. And when they had kindled a fire in the midst of the hall, and were set down together, Peter sat down among them. But a certain maid beheld him as he sat by the fire, and earnestly looked upon him, and said, This man was also with him. And he denied him, saying, Woman, I know him not.

And after a little while another saw him, and said, Thou art also of them. And Peter said, Man, I am not. And about the space of one hour after another confidently affirmed, saying, Of a truth this fellow also was with him: for he is a Galilæan. And Peter said, Man, I know not what thou sayest. And immediately, while he yet spake, the cock crew.

And the Lord turned, and looked upon Peter. And Peter remembered the word of the Lord, how he had said unto him, Before the cock crow, thou shalt deny me thrice. And Peter went out, and wept bitterly.

Luke xxii.54-62

THE COCK

Cocks may have been brought to Palestine by the Romans. They were used for food, and also for the sport of cock-fighting.

CHARCOAL FIRE

In the Middle East, houses did not have fireplaces. On cold nights, a brazier would be lit to give warmth. The fuel was charcoal or dung.

THE SYMBOL OF ST. PETER

Peter, one of the three favourite disciples of Jesus, is often shown holding keys. These are meant to be the keys of Heaven.

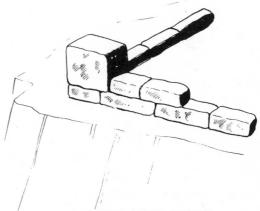

PETER—THE ROCK

Peter was given this name by Jesus.

It was the custom to place cornerstones and foundations of buildings upon rock, because of its strength.

The story in the text shows Peter in his weakest moment. After the death of Jesus, he became strong in his faith, and was the leader of the early Christians.

TRIAL BEFORE PILATE

And straightway in the morning the chief priests held a consultation with the elders and scribes and the whole council, and bound Jesus, and carried him away, and delivered him to Pilate. And Pilate asked him, Art thou the King of the Jews? And he answering said unto him, Thou sayest it. And the chief priests accused him of many things: but he answered nothing.

And Pilate asked him again, saying, Answerest thou nothing? behold how many things they witness against thee. But Jesus yet answered nothing; so that Pilate marvelled.

Now at that feast he released unto them one prisoner, whomsoever they desired. And there was one named Barabbas, which lay bound with them that had made insurrection with him, who had committed murder in the insurrection. And the multitude crying aloud began to desire him to do as he had ever done unto them. But Pilate answered them, saying, Will ye that I release unto you the King of the Jews? For he knew that the chief priests had delivered him for envy. But the chief priests moved the people, that he should rather release Barabbas unto them. And Pilate answered and said again unto them, What will ye then that I shall do unto him whom ye call the King of the Jews? And they cried out again, Crucify him. Then Pilate said unto them, Why, what evil hath he done? And they cried out the more exceedingly, Crucify him.

And so Pilate, willing to content the people, released Barabbas unto them, and delivered Jesus, when he had scourged him, to be crucified.

Mark xv.1-15

156

THE SANHEDRIN
The chief court of the Jews. It had 71 members. They could punish anyone who broke Jewish law, if the Roman governor agreed. After the Sanhedrin had found Jesus guilty and sentenced him to death, they took him to Pilate for his agreement.

"TO WASH ONE'S HANDS"
These words are still used when a person will have nothing to do with a plan.

Pontius Pilate tried Jesus, and found that he had done nothing wrong. The priests still wanted Jesus to die. Pilate washed his hands before the crowd and said, "I am innocent of the blood of this just person."

PILATE WASHING HIS HANDS

THE CRUCIFIXION

And the soldiers led him away into the hall, called Prætorium; and they call together the whole band. And they clothed him with purple, and plaited a crown of thorns, and put it about his head, and began to salute him, Hail, King of the Jews! And they smote him on the head with a reed, and did spit upon him, and bowing their knees worshipped him. And when they had mocked him, they took off the purple from him, and put his own clothes on him, and led him out to crucify him.

And they compel one Simon a Cyrenian, who passed by, coming out of the country, the father of Alexander and Rufus, to bear his cross. And they bring him unto the place Golgotha, which is, being interpreted, the place of a skull. And they gave him to drink wine mingled with myrrh: but he received it not. And when they had crucified him, they parted his garments, casting lots upon them, what every man should take.

And it was the third hour, and they crucified him. And the superscription of his accusation was written over, THE KING OF THE JEWS. And with him they crucify two thieves; the one on his right hand, and the other on his left. And the scripture was fulfilled, which saith, And he was numbered with the transgressors.

And they that passed by railed on him, wagging their heads, and saying, Ah, thou that destroyest the temple, and buildest it in three days, save thyself, and come down from the cross. Likewise also the chief priests mocking said among themselves with the scribes, He saved others; himself he cannot save. Let Christ the King of Israel descend now from the cross, that we may see and believe. And they that were crucified with him reviled him. And when the sixth hour was come, there was darkness over the whole land until the ninth hour.

And at the ninth hour Jesus cried with a loud voice, saying, Eloi, Eloi, lama sabachthani? which is, being interpreted, My God, my God, why hast thou forsaken me? And some of them that stood by, when they heard it, said, Behold, he calleth Elias.

And one ran and filled a sponge full of vinegar, and put it on a reed, and gave him to drink, saying, Let alone; let us see whether Elias will come to take him down. And Jesus cried with a loud voice, and gave up the ghost. And the veil of the temple was rent in twain from the top to the bottom.

And when the centurion, which stood over against him, saw that he so cried out, and gave up the ghost, he said, Truly this man was the Son of God.

Mark xv.16-39

THE NOTICE ON THE CROSS

The letters stood for these four Latin words: *IESUS NAZARENUS REX IUDAEORUM*. They mean "Jesus of Nazareth, King of the Jews." There are no "J"s in Latin, and Pilate used the letter "I".

"THE CROWN OF THORNS"

Generals and emperors were often crowned with a garland of laurels. The soldiers mocked Jesus, by giving him a garland of thorns.

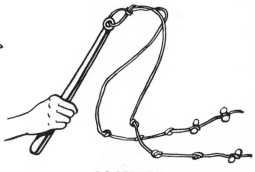

SCOURGE

Jesus was scourged before being crucified. This was the usual custom.

MYRRH

The gum from this tree was mixed with wine to make a drug to deaden pain.

THE VEIL OF THE TEMPLE

This was a curtain in front of the Holy of Holies in the temple.

Only priests were allowed to pass through the veil, to talk to God.

The tearing of the veil showed that everyone could now get close to God.

VINEGAR

Vinegar was sour wine mixed with water. It was a drink of the Roman soldiers.

THE EMBALMMENT AND BURIAL OF JESUS

There were also women looking on afar off: among whom was Mary Magdalene, and Mary the mother of James the less and of Joses, and Salome; (Who also, when he was in Galilee, followed him, and ministered unto him;) and many other women which came up with him unto Jerusalem.

And now when the even was come, because it was the preparation, that is, the day before the sabbath, Joseph of Arimathæa, an honourable counsellor, which also waited for the kingdom of God, came, and went in boldly unto Pilate, and craved the body of Jesus.

And Pilate marvelled if he were already dead: and calling unto him the centurion, he asked him whether he had been any while dead. And when he knew it of the centurion, he gave the body to Joseph. And he bought fine linen, and took him down, and wrapped him in the linen, and laid him in a sepulchre which was hewn out of a rock, and rolled a stone unto the door of the sepulchre. And Mary Magdalene and Mary the mother of Joses beheld where he was laid.

Mark xv.40-47

JOSEPH OF ARIMATHÆA
It is said that Joseph was a merchant who traded with Britain. An old legend tells us that he came for tin and little shell-fish from which purple dyes were made. On one of his voyages he brought with him the boy Jesus.

The lines of the hymn "Jerusalem" refer to this legend.

THE TOMB OF JESUS
The tomb probably looked like this from the outside. The opening was covered by a round stone like a millstone.

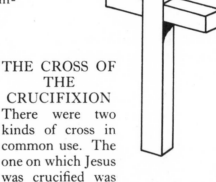

THE CROSS OF THE CRUCIFIXION
There were two kinds of cross in common use. The one on which Jesus was crucified was probably like this, because we are told that a notice was placed above his head. The other kind of cross was T-shaped.

CELTIC CROSS
A very early cross in Britain and Ireland. The circle means everlasting life.

CANTERBURY CROSS
A typical cross used on some English altars.

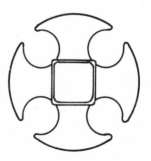

The cross on which Jesus died has become the symbol of Christian churches all over the world.

THE EMPTY TOMB

And when the sabbath was past, Mary Magdalene, and Mary the mother of James, and Salome, had brought sweet spices, that they might come and anoint him. And very early in the morning the first day of the week, they came unto the sepulchre at the rising of the sun. And they said among themselves, Who shall roll us away the stone from the door of the sepulchre? And when they looked, they saw that the stone was rolled away: for it was very great. And entering into the sepulchre, they saw a young man sitting on the right side, clothed in a long white garment; and they were affrighted. And he saith unto them, Be not affrighted: Ye seek Jesus of Nazareth, which was crucified: he is risen; he is not here: behold the place where they laid him. But go your way, tell his disciples and Peter that he goeth before you into Galilee: there shall ye see him, as he said unto you.

And they went out quickly, and fled from the sepulchre; for they trembled and were amazed: neither said they any thing to any man; for they were afraid.

Mark xvi.1-8

SIMON PETER
Preached to the Jews, and was crucified head downwards in Rome, A.D. 68.

JOHN
Preached in Asia Minor. Lived in Ephesus, and wrote five books of the Bible. He died about A.D. 100.

PHILIP
Preached in Palestine and Asia Minor, where he was stoned to death by the priests of the serpent-worshippers. His symbol is two loaves of bread.

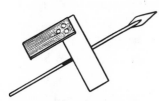

THOMAS
Preached in Syria, Persia, and India. He was killed by a shower of arrows while praying.

ANDREW
Preached in Greece, Russia, and Asia Minor. He was crucified at Patrae, on the cross which is used as his symbol.

JAMES THE LESS
Little is known of him. He may have preached in Egypt. It is said that he was sawn to death.

THE APOSTLES
These symbols are to be found in many stained-glass windows. They are a way of naming the apostle.

BARTHOLOMEW
Nothing is known of his work. His symbols are a flaying knife and a Bible. By tradition he was flayed to death in Armenia. He may be the Nathanael in the Gospel of St. John.

SIMON
(THE ZEALOT)
Simon and Jude went together. It is said that they were two of the shepherds who came to Bethlehem for the birth of Jesus. There is a story that Simon was crucified.

JAMES THE ELDER
The first apostle to be killed. He was beheaded by Herod, A.D. 44. A pilgrim's staff and wallet show that he was a traveller. He went to Spain.

JUDE
(THADDÆUS)
He is supposed to have preached in Assyria and Persia. It is said that he was clubbed to death by Persians, about A.D. 80.

MATTHEW (LEVI)
He preached and died in Ethiopia. The money-bags show that he was a tax-collector.

JUDAS
His symbol is a blank shield of yellow. He killed himself after betraying Jesus.

JESUS AND MARY MAGDALENE

But Mary stood without at the sepulchre weeping: and as she wept, she stooped down, and looked into the sepulchre, and seeth two angels in white sitting, the one at the head, and the other at the feet, where the body of Jesus had lain. And they say unto her, Woman, why weepest thou? She saith unto them, Because they have taken away my Lord, and I know not where they have laid him.

And when she had thus said, she turned herself back, and saw Jesus standing, and knew not that it was Jesus. Jesus saith unto her, Woman, why weepest thou? whom seekest thou? She, supposing him to be the gardener, saith unto him, Sir, if thou have borne him hence, tell me where thou hast laid him, and I will take him away. Jesus saith unto her, Mary. She turned herself, and saith unto him, Rabboni; which is to say, Master.

Jesus saith unto her, Touch me not; for I am not yet ascended to my Father: but go to my brethren, and say unto them, I ascend unto my Father, and your Father; and to my God, and your God.

Mary Magdalene came and told the disciples that she had seen the Lord, and that he had spoken these things unto her.

John xx.11-18

THE DOORWAY TO THE CHURCH OF THE HOLY SEPULCHRE

This church was built where it was believed that Jesus had been buried. Over the door are carved pictures of scenes from the New Testament.

THE WAILING WALL

Jews go to the Wailing Wall, which is all that is left of the temple of Solomon. It is a very sacred spot to the Jews. They mourn the loss of their holy places.

The Moslems have built a mosque on the ground where king Solomon's temple once stood.

THE CHAPEL OF CALVARY

A chapel has been built on the place where Jesus was crucified.

JERUSALEM

Jerusalem is a holy city to Jews, Christians, and Mohammedans.

For the Jews, it is the place where the temple once stood.

For the Christians, it is the place where Jesus was crucified and buried.

For the Mohammedans, it is the place where Abraham worshipped and which Mohammed visited.

EMMAUS

And, behold, two of them went that same day to a village called Emmaus, which was from Jerusalem about threescore furlongs. And they talked together of all these things which had happened. And it came to pass, that, while they communed together and reasoned, Jesus himself drew near, and went with them. But their eyes were holden that they should not know him. And he said unto them, What manner of communications are these that ye have to one another, as ye walk, and are sad? And the one of them, whose name was Cleopas, answering said unto him, Art thou only a stranger in Jerusalem, and hast not known the things which are come to pass there in these days? And he said unto them, What things? And they said unto him, Concerning Jesus of Nazareth, which was a prophet mighty in deed and word before God and all the people: and how the chief priests and our rulers delivered him to be condemned to death, and have crucified him. But we trusted that it had been he which should have redeemed Israel: and beside all this, to day is the third day since these things were done. Yea, and certain women also of our company made us astonished, which were early at the sepulchre. And when they found not his body, they came, saying, that they had also seen a vision of angels, which said that he was alive. And certain of them which were with us went to the sepulchre, and found it even so as the women had said: but him they saw not.

Then he said unto them, O fools, and slow of heart to believe all that the prophets have spoken: ought not Christ to have suffered these things, and to enter into his glory? And beginning at Moses and all the prophets, he expounded unto them in all the scriptures the things concerning himself.

And they drew nigh unto the village, whither they went: and he made as though he would have gone further. But they constrained him, saying, Abide with us: for it is toward evening, and the day is far spent: And he went in to tarry with them. And it came to pass, as he sat at meat with them, he took bread, and blessed it, and brake, and gave to them. And their eyes were opened, and they knew him; and he vanished out of their sight.

And they said one to another, Did not our heart burn within us, while he talked with us by the way, and while he opened to us the scriptures?

And they rose up the same hour, and returned to Jerusalem, and found the eleven gathered together, and them that were with them, saying, The Lord is risen indeed, and hath appeared to Simon. And they told what things were done in the way, and how he was known of them in breaking of bread.

Luke xxiv.13-35

THE BREAKING OF BREAD

The two friends who met Jesus on the road to Emmaus did not know him until they began to eat.

When Jesus broke the bread, they knew him by the way he did it.

THE GATE OF THE GARDENS

The disciples, on their way to Emmaus, probably left Jerusalem by this gate. The level of the city has now almost reached the top of the arch.

This picture shows how archaeologists have to dig deeply to find traces of the old city.

"and hath appeared unto Simon"

There are no stories in the Bible telling of this meeting.

It is mentioned in the story of the journey to Emmaus, and by Paul in 1 Corinthians xv.5.

From this time onwards, Simon Peter was the leader of the people who believed in Jesus Christ.

THOMAS, THE DOUBTER

But Thomas, one of the twelve, called Didymus, was not with them when Jesus came. The other disciples therefore said unto him, We have seen the Lord. But he said unto them, Except I shall see in his hands the print of the nails, and put my finger into the print of the nails, and thrust my hand into his side, I will not believe.

And after eight days again his disciples were within, and Thomas with them: then came Jesus, the doors being shut, and stood in the midst, and said, Peace be unto you. Then saith he to Thomas, Reach hither thy finger, and behold my hands; and reach hither thy hand, and thrust it into my side: and be not faithless, but believing. And Thomas answered and said unto him, My Lord and my God. Jesus saith unto him, Thomas, because thou hast seen me, thou hast believed: blessed are they that have not seen, and yet have believed.

John xx.24-29

JESUS BY THE SEA OF GALILEE

After these things Jesus shewed himself again to the disciples at the sea of Tiberias; and on this wise shewed he himself. There were together Simon Peter, and Thomas called Didymus, and Nathanael of Cana in Galilee, and the sons of Zebedee, and two other of his disciples. Simon Peter saith unto them, I go a fishing. They say unto him, We also go with thee. They went forth, and that night they caught nothing. But when the morning was now come, Jesus stood on the shore: but the disciples knew not that it was Jesus. Then Jesus saith unto them, Children, have ye any meat? They answered him, No. And he said unto them, Cast the net on the right side of the ship, and ye shall find. They cast therefore, and now they were not able to draw it for the multitude of fishes. Therefore that disciple whom Jesus loved saith unto Peter, It is the Lord. Now when Simon Peter heard that it was the Lord, he girt his fisher's coat unto him, (for he was naked,) and did cast himself into the sea. And the other disciples came in a little ship; (for they were not far from land, but as it were two hundred cubits,) dragging the net with fishes. As soon then as they were come to land they saw a fire of coals there, and fish laid thereon, and bread. Jesus saith unto them, Bring of the fish which ye have now caught. Simon Peter went up, and drew the net to land full of great fishes, an hundred and fifty and three: and for all there were so many, yet was not the net broken. Jesus saith unto them, Come and dine. And none of the disciples durst ask him, Who art thou? knowing that it was the Lord. Jesus then cometh, and taketh bread, and giveth them, and fish likewise. This is now the third time that Jesus shewed himself to his disciples, after that he was risen from the dead.

So when they had dined, Jesus saith to Simon Peter, Simon, son of Jonas, lovest thou me more than these? He saith unto him, Yea, Lord; thou knowest that I love thee. He saith unto him, Feed my lambs.

He saith to him again the second time, Simon, son of Jonas, lovest thou me? He saith unto him, Yea, Lord; thou knowest that I love thee. He saith unto him, Feed my sheep.

He saith unto him the third time, Simon, son of Jonas, lovest thou me? Peter was grieved because he said unto him the third time, Lovest thou me? And he said unto him, Lord, thou knowest all things; thou knowest that I love thee. Jesus saith unto him, Feed my sheep. Verily, verily, I say unto thee, When thou wast young, thou girdedst thyself, and walkedst whither thou wouldest: but when thou shalt be old, thou shalt stretch forth thy hands, and another shall gird thee, and carry thee whither thou wouldest not.

This spake he, signifying by what death he should glorify God. And when he had spoken this, he saith unto him, Follow me.

Then Peter, turning about, seeth the disciple whom Jesus loved following; which also leaned on his breast at supper, and said, Lord, which is he that betrayeth thee? Peter seeing him saith to Jesus, Lord, and what shall this man do? Jesus saith unto him, If I will that he tarry till I come, what is that to thee? Follow thou me.

Then went this saying abroad among the brethren, that that disciple should not die: yet Jesus said not unto him, He shall not die; but, If I will that he tarry till I come, what is that to thee?

John xxi.1-23

THE ASCENSION

So then after the Lord had spoken unto them, he was received up into heaven, and sat on the right hand of God.

And they went forth, and preached every where, the Lord working with them, and confirming the word with signs following.

Mark xvi.19, 20

DOMINE, QUO VADIS?

An old story tells us that, when Peter was leaving Rome, because the emperor was killing all the Christians there, he met Jesus walking towards the city and carrying his cross. Peter said, "Domine, quo vadis?"—which meant, "Master, where are you going?" Jesus answered that he was going to Rome, to be crucified again.

Peter, ashamed that he had been running away from danger, returned to Rome and was crucified.

ST. PETER'S CHURCH, ROME

The Church of St. Peter stands on the spot where he is believed to have been put to death. It was built between the years 1506 and 1626. Its dome was designed by the great sculptor Michelangelo. He would take no reward for this work, because he wished to do it for the glory of God. He died before it was finished.

*PENTECOST

And when the day of Pentecost was fully come, they were all with one accord in one place. And suddenly there came a sound from heaven as of a rushing mighty wind, and it filled all the house where they were sitting. And there appeared unto them cloven tongues like as of fire, and it sat upon each of them. And they were all filled with the Holy Ghost, and began to speak with other tongues, as the Spirit gave them utterance.

And there were dwelling at Jerusalem Jews, devout men, out of every nation under heaven. And they were all amazed and marvelled, saying one to another, Behold, are not all these which speak Galilæans? And how hear we every man in our own tongue, wherein we were born? Others mocking said, These men are full of new wine.

But Peter, standing up with the eleven, lifted up his voice, and said unto them, Ye men of Judæa, and all ye that dwell at Jerusalem, be this known unto you, and hearken to my words: for these are not drunken, as ye suppose, seeing it is but the third hour of the day. But this is that which was spoken by the prophet Joel; and it shall come to pass in the last days, saith God, I will pour out of my Spirit upon all flesh: and your sons and your daughters shall prophesy, and your young men shall see visions, and your old men shall dream dreams: and on my servants and on my handmaidens I will pour out in those days of my Spirit; and they shall prophesy. And I will shew wonders in heaven above, and signs in the earth beneath; blood, and fire, and vapour of smoke. The sun shall be turned into darkness, and the moon into blood, before that great and notable day of the Lord come: and it shall come to pass that whosoever shall call on the name of the Lord shall be saved. Ye men of Israel, hear these words; Jesus of Nazareth, a man approved of God among you by miracles and wonders and signs, which God did by him in the midst of you, as ye yourselves also know: him ye have taken, and by wicked hands have crucified and slain. This Jesus hath God raised up, whereof we all are witnesses. Therefore, being by the right hand of God exalted, and having received of the Father the promise of the Holy Ghost, he hath shed forth this, which ye now see and hear. Therefore let all the house of Israel know assuredly, that God hath made that same Jesus, whom ye have crucified, both Lord and Christ.

Now when they heard this, they were pricked in their heart, and said unto Peter and to the rest of the apostles, Men and brethren, what shall we do? Then Peter said unto them, Repent, and be baptised every one of you in the name of Jesus Christ for the remission of sins, and ye shall receive the gift of the Holy Ghost.

Then they that gladly received his word were baptized: and the same day there were added unto them about three thousand souls. And they continued stedfastly in the apostles' doctrine and fellowship, and in breaking of bread, and in prayers.

Acts ii

THE FIRST MIRACLE

Now Peter and John went together into the temple at the hour of prayer being the ninth hour. And a certain man lame from his mother's womb was carried, whom they laid daily at the gate of the temple which is called Beautiful, to ask alms of them that entered into the temple; who seeing Peter and John about to go into the temple asked an alms. And Peter, fastening his eyes upon him with John, said, Look on us. Silver and gold have I none; but such as I have give I thee: In the name of Jesus Christ of Nazareth rise up and walk. And he took him by the right hand, and lifted him up: and immediately his feet and ancle bones received strength. And he leaping up stood and walked, and entered with them into the temple, walking, and leaping, and praising God. And all the people saw him, and were filled with wonder and amazement at that which had happened unto him.

And when Peter saw it, he answered unto the people, Ye men of Israel, why marvel ye at this? or why look ye so earnestly on us, as though by our own power or holiness we had made this man to walk? The God of Abraham, and of Isaac, and of Jacob, the God of our fathers, hath glorified his Son Jesus; whom ye delivered up, and denied him in the presence of Pilate, when he was determined to let him go. But ye denied the Holy One and the Just, and desired a murderer to be granted unto you; and killed the Prince of life, whom God hath raised from the dead; whereof we are witnesses. And his name through faith in his name hath made this man strong, whom ye see and know: yea, the faith which is by him hath given him this perfect soundness in the presence of you all. And now, brethren, I wot that through ignorance ye did it, as did also your rulers. But those things which God before had shewed by the mouth of all his prophets that Christ should suffer, he hath so fulfilled.

Repent ye therefore, and be converted, that your sins may be blotted out, when the times of refreshing shall come from the presence of the Lord; and he shall send Jesus Christ, which before was preached unto you: whom the heaven must receive until the times of restitution of all things, which God hath spoken by the mouth of all his holy prophets since the world began. For Moses truly said unto the fathers, A prophet shall the Lord your God raise up unto you of your brethren, like unto me; him shall ye hear in all things whatsoever he shall say unto you. And it shall come to pass, that every soul, which will not hear that prophet, shall be destroyed from among the people. Yea, and all the prophets from Samuel and those that follow after, as many as have spoken, have likewise foretold of these days. Ye are the children of the prophets, and of the covenant which God made with our fathers, saying unto Abraham, And in thy seed shall all the kindreds of the earth be blessed. Unto you first God, having raised up his Son Jesus, sent him to bless you, in turning away every one of you from his iniquities.

Acts iii

ALMS

People unable to earn their living had to beg for food and money. They sat in places where many people would come.

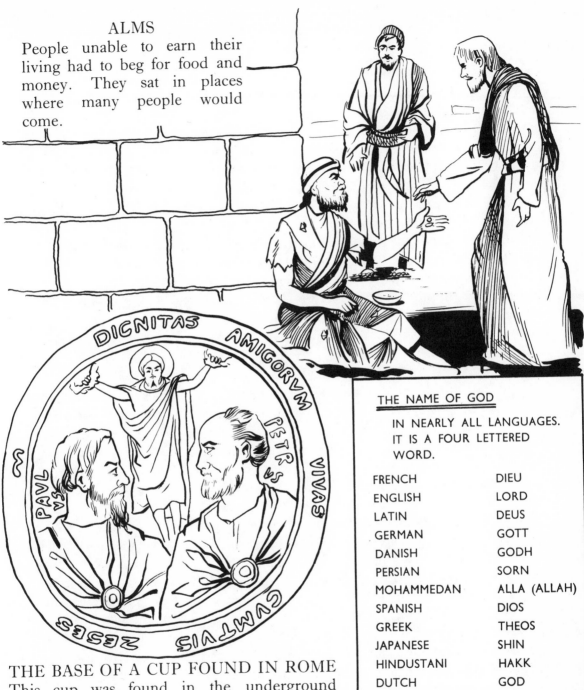

THE BASE OF A CUP FOUND IN ROME
This cup was found in the underground passages of Rome, where the Christians hid from the emperor Nero. The two persons shown are said to be Peter and Paul.

THE NAME OF GOD

IN NEARLY ALL LANGUAGES. IT IS A FOUR LETTERED WORD.

FRENCH	DIEU
ENGLISH	LORD
LATIN	DEUS
GERMAN	GOTT
DANISH	GODH
PERSIAN	SORN
MOHAMMEDAN	ALLA (ALLAH)
SPANISH	DIOS
GREEK	THEOS
JAPANESE	SHIN
HINDUSTANI	HAKK
DUTCH	GOD

IMPRISONMENT AND ESCAPE

Now about that time Herod the king stretched forth his hands to vex certain of the church. And he killed James the brother of John with the sword. And because he saw it pleased the Jews, he proceeded further to take Peter also. (Then were the days of unleavened bread.) And when he had apprehended him, he put him in prison, and delivered him to four quaternions of soldiers to keep him; intending after Easter to bring him forth to the people. Peter therefore was kept in prison: but prayer was made without ceasing of the church unto God for him.

And when Herod would have brought him forth, the same night Peter was sleeping between two soldiers, bound with two chains: and the keepers before the door kept the prison. And, behold, the angel of the Lord came upon him, and a light shined in the prison: and he smote Peter on the side, and raised him up, saying, Arise up quickly. And his chains fell off from his hands. And the angel said unto him, Gird thyself, and bind on thy sandals. And so he did. And he saith unto him, Cast thy garment about thee, and follow me. And he went out, and followed him; and wist not that it was true which was done by the angel; but thought he saw a vision. When they were past the first and the second ward, they came unto the iron gate that leadeth unto the city; which opened to them of his own accord: and they went out, and passed on through one street; and forthwith the angel departed from him. And when Peter was come to himself, he said, Now I know of a surety, that the Lord hath sent his angel, and hath delivered me out of the hand of Herod, and from all the expectation of the people of the Jews.

And when he had considered the thing, he came to the house of Mary the mother of John, whose surname was Mark; where many were gathered together praying. And as Peter knocked at the door of the gate, a damsel came to hearken, named Rhoda. And when she knew Peter's voice, she opened not the gate for gladness, but ran in, and told how Peter stood before the gate. And they said unto her, Thou art mad. But she constantly affirmed that it was even so. Then said they, It is his angel. But Peter continued knocking: and when they had opened the door, and saw him, they were astonished. But he, beckoning unto them with the hand to hold their peace, declared unto them how the Lord had brought him out of the prison. And he said, Go shew these things unto James, and to the brethren. And he departed, and went into another place.

Acts xii.1-17

PETER AND THE QUATERNION

Peter was guarded by a quaternion, that is, four Roman soldiers who did one of the four night watches. Two were chained to Peter, and one stood at each of the two doors of the prison.

These two were known as the first and second ward.

THE HOUSE OF MARY

Peter went often to Mary's house. Mary's son, John Mark, became a Christian. He wrote the Gospel according to St. Mark.

He travelled with Paul and Barnabas, and was with Paul in Rome. He may have been the young man who was present when Jesus was taken by the Jews.

RHODA
AT THE DOOR

Rhoda was probably a young servant girl or relative of the family.

THE MARTYRDOM OF STEPHEN

[Stephen was brought before the high priest and charged with the crime of blasphemy, for the priests said that he had spoken against the law of Moses. The council saw before them a saintly-looking man. The charge was read to Stephen and the high priest said, "Is it true that you have spoken these words?"

Stephen replied, "Men, brethren and fathers, The God of glory appeared unto Abraham, and he was told to go from Mesopotamia to Charran, and then from Charran to the land in which you now live. God then said that the people would be taken prisoner for four hundred years and then they would be free and live in this place. Abraham had a son Isaac, Isaac had a son Jacob, and Jacob had twelve sons who were to become the patriarchs.

"The patriarchs sold Joseph into slavery in Egypt, but God was with him, and, at the time of the great famine in Egypt and Canaan, Joseph, who had become a great man in Egypt, called his father and his family to Egypt where they settled.

"Then another ruler came to the throne who was harsh to the people of Israel. His daughter found a small baby whom she had brought up as her own. This child was Moses. He had to flee from Egypt because he killed a man who was ill-treating an Israelite, but after forty years he received the word of God and went back to Egypt to lead his people out of slavery. This was the man Moses whom the people of Israel at first refused, saying, 'Who made you a ruler and a judge?' It was Moses that said, 'A prophet shall the Lord your God raise up unto you of your brethren, like unto me; him shall ye hear.' The people of Israel often refused to listen to Moses. There was a time when they wished to turn back to Egypt. There was another time when they built a golden calf and worshipped idols. Throughout the story of the people of Israel there are times when they have not listened to the word of God. You are the same as your fathers. Your fathers slew the prophets and those that told of the coming of the Just One. You have now become murderers and betrayers. You, who have received messages from angels, have not obeyed."

When the priests heard what Stephen had to say they were very angry but he seemed to take no notice of their anger. Instead he looked up towards heaven. Then he said, "Behold, I see the heavens opened, and the Son of man standing on the right hand of God." They roughly seized him and dragged him away to the edge of the town where he would suffer death by stoning. As the dreadful punishment took place, Stephen knelt and in a loud clear voice said, "Lord Jesus receive my spirit and lay not this sin to their charge."]

Acts vii

THE STONING OF STEPHEN

Stoning was the death for blasphemy and idolatry. The crowd covered their ears when Stephen told them of his vision of Jesus standing by the side of God. The mob killed Stephen without asking the Romans. The young man looking after the clothes was Saul who later became Paul.

STEPHEN'S GATE JERUSALEM

This was supposed to have been the gate through which Stephen was led to his death.

STEPHEN GIVING TO THE POOR

The Apostles chose seven men to take care of poor Christians. These men were the *Deacons*. Their work gave the Apostles more time for teaching. Stephen was probably a Greek Jew. He was made a Deacon, and was the first man to die for Jesus.

THE ROAD TO DAMASCUS

Saul, breathing out threatenings and slaughter against the disciples of the Lord, went unto the high priest, and desired of him letters to Damascus to the synagogues, that if he found any of this way, whether they were men or women, he might bring them bound unto Jerusalem.

As he journeyed, he came near Damascus: and suddenly there shined round about him a light from heaven. He fell to the earth, and heard a voice saying unto him, Saul, Saul, why persecutest thou me? He, trembling and astonished, said, Who art thou, Lord? The Lord said, I am Jesus whom thou persecutest: it is hard for thee to kick against the pricks. He, trembling and astonished said, Lord, what wilt thou have me do? The Lord said unto him, Arise, and go into the city, and it shall be told thee what thou must do. The men which journeyed with him stood speechless, hearing a voice, but seeing no man.

Saul arose from the earth; and when his eyes were opened he saw no man. They led him by the hand and brought him into Damascus.

Acts ix.1-8

SAUL

Saul was the right man for this missionary work, because:

(1) He was an intelligent man.

(2) He spoke Greek, which was the language of Asia Minor, and he knew Greek customs.

(3) He was a Roman citizen, and so could travel freely within the Roman empire.

(4) As a Pharisee, he knew the Scriptures and could talk to Jews.

GREEKS IN TARSUS

Saul went to school in Tarsus. He learned Greek, and Greek customs.

WHERE SAUL LIVED

Saul was born in Tarsus. Tarsus was a Roman city, and so Saul was a citizen of Rome.

THE TRADE OF A TENTMAKER

Saul's father was a tentmaker. He also made sails, awnings, and cloaks of camel-hair. This may have been Saul's trade. He was a rich man.

STUDYING AT JERUSALEM

Saul was a Pharisee. At the age of twenty he went to Jerusalem to study Jewish law and religion. He was taught by Gamaliel, a great Jewish teacher.

*JUPITER AND MERCURY

Paul and Barnabas fled to Lystra and Derbe, cities of Lycaonia, and there they preached the gospel. There sat a certain man at Lystra who never had walked. Paul, perceiving that he had faith to be healed, said with a loud voice, Stand upright on thy feet. And he leaped and walked.

When the people saw what Paul had done, they lifted up their voices saying, The gods are come down to us in the likeness of men. They called Barnabas, Jupiter; and Paul, Mercurius, because he was the chief speaker. Then the priest of Jupiter, which was before their city, brought oxen and garlands unto the gates and would have done sacrifice with the people. When the apostles Barnabas and Paul heard, they rent their clothes, and ran in among the people crying out, Sirs, why do ye these things? We also are men of like passions with you, and preach unto you that ye should turn from these vanities unto the living God, which made heaven, and earth, and the sea, and all things that are therein: who in times past suffered all nations to walk in their own ways. Nevertheless he left not himself without witness, in that he did good, and gave us rain from heaven, and fruitful seasons, filling our hearts with food and gladness. With these sayings scarce restrained they the people, that they had not done sacrifice unto them.

And there came thither certain Jews from Antioch and Iconium, who persuaded the people, and, having stoned Paul, drew him out of the city, supposing he had been dead. Howbeit, as the disciples stood round about him, he rose up, and came into the city. The next day he departed with Barnabas to Derbe.

Acts xiv.6-20

A WARNING

[Once, while Paul was staying at the house of Philip, there came a prophet from Judæa called Agabus. He took Paul's girdle and bound his own arms and feet and said, "Thus saith the Holy Ghost. So shall the Jews at Jerusalem bind the man that owneth this girdle, and shall deliver him into the hands of the Gentiles." When the others heard these words they begged Paul not to go to Jerusalem, but he answered, "Why are you trying to make me change my mind? I am not only ready to be bound, but also to die for the name of the Lord Jesus." Everyone soon saw that Paul would not change his mind and they no longer tried to stop him going.]

Acts xxi.8-14

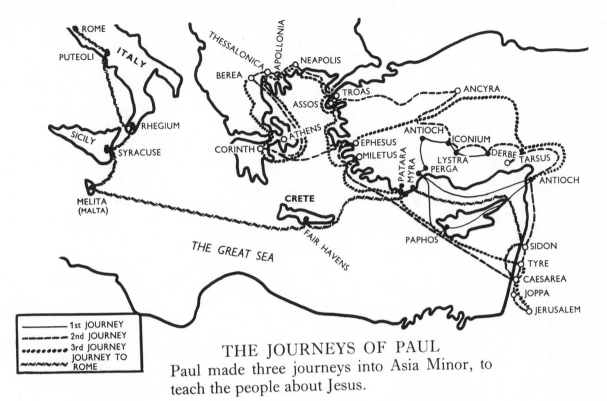

THE JOURNEYS OF PAUL

Paul made three journeys into Asia Minor, to teach the people about Jesus.

MERCURY

Mercury, or Hermes, was the messenger of the gods.

JUPITER

Jupiter, or Zeus, was the chief of the Greek and Roman gods.

The story told here took place during the first missionary journey.

THE ARREST

The Jews which were of Asia, when they saw him in the temple, stirred up all the people, and laid hands on him, crying out, Men of Israel, help: this is the man that teacheth all men every where against the people, and the law, and this place: and further brought Greeks also into the temple, and hath polluted this holy place. (They had seen an Ephesian whom they supposed Paul had brought into the temple.) All the city was moved, and the people ran together: and they took Paul, and drew him out of the temple: and forthwith the doors were shut.

As they went about to kill him, tidings came unto the chief captain of the band, that all Jerusalem was in an uproar, who immediately took soldiers and centurions and ran down unto them. When they saw the chief captain and the soldiers, they left beating Paul. The chief captain came near and took him, and commanded him to be bound with two chains; demanded who he was, and what he had done. Some cried one thing, some another, and when he could not know the certainty for the tumult, he commanded him to be carried into the castle. The multitude of the people followed crying, Away with him.

As Paul was to be led into the castle he said unto the chief captain, May I speak unto thee? I am a man which am a Jew of Tarsus, a city in Cilicia, a citizen of no mean city. I beseech thee, suffer me to speak unto the people.

Paul stood on the stairs, and when there was a great silence he spake unto them.

Acts xxi.27-40

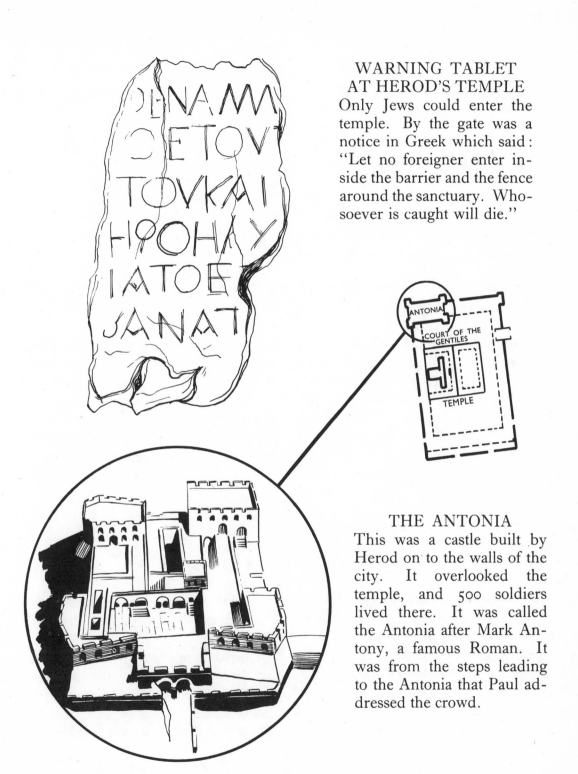

WARNING TABLET AT HEROD'S TEMPLE

Only Jews could enter the temple. By the gate was a notice in Greek which said: "Let no foreigner enter inside the barrier and the fence around the sanctuary. Whosoever is caught will die."

ANTONIA

COURT OF THE GENTILES

TEMPLE

THE ANTONIA

This was a castle built by Herod on to the walls of the city. It overlooked the temple, and 500 soldiers lived there. It was called the Antonia after Mark Antony, a famous Roman. It was from the steps leading to the Antonia that Paul addressed the crowd.

APPEAL TO CÆSAR

Now when Festus was come into the province, after three days he ascended from Cæsarea to Jerusalem. Then the high priest and the chief of the Jews informed him against Paul, and besought him, and desired favour against him, that he would send for him to Jerusalem, laying wait in the way to kill him. But Festus answered, that Paul should be kept at Cæsarea, and that he himself would depart shortly thither.

Let them therefore, said he, which among you are able, go down with me, and accuse this man, if there be any wickedness in him. When he had tarried among them more than ten days, he went down unto Cæsarea; and the next day sitting on the judgment seat commanded Paul to be brought. When he was come, the Jews which came down from Jerusalem stood round about, and laid many and grievous complaints against Paul, which they could not prove. He answered, Neither against the law of the Jews, neither against the temple, nor yet against Cæsar, have I offended. Festus, willing to do the Jews a pleasure, answered Paul, and said, Wilt thou go up to Jerusalem, and there be judged of these things before me? Then said Paul, I stand at Cæsar's judgment seat, where I ought to be judged: to the Jews have I done no wrong, as thou very well knowest. For if I be an offender, or have committed any thing worthy of death, I refuse not to die: but if there be none of these things whereof these accuse me, no man may deliver me unto them. I appeal unto Cæsar.

Then Festus, when he had conferred with the council, answered, Hast thou appealed unto Cæsar? unto Cæsar shalt thou go.

Acts xxv.1-12

THE SHIPWRECK

[When it had been decided that the journey should be made to Italy, Paul and the other prisoners were placed in the custody of Julius, a centurion in Augustus's army. It was intended that they should follow the coast of Asia because they had a guide with them who came from Macedonia.

The second day out the ship stopped at Sidon. Here the centurion very kindly allowed Paul to go ashore and meet some friends. After leaving Sidon the winds were often contrary and the ship was blown off course, so that they were forced to go around by way of Cyprus and across the Seas of Cilicia and Pamphylia to Myra, a city in Lycia.

THE JUDGMENT SEAT

A bench on which the governor sat in order to give an official verdict when trying a case.

> *"I appeal unto Cæsar"*
> A Roman citizen had the right to be tried by the highest court in the Roman empire. This was at the judgment seat of Cæsar in Rome.
>
> Paul knew that he would not be treated fairly in Jerusalem, so he claimed his right as a Roman citizen.

NERO

Paul asked to be tried before Cæsar. The Cæsar he spoke of was the emperor Nero. Nero killed many Christians, because he blamed them for the great fire in Rome. It is said that he played the fiddle while Rome burned.

A CENTURION

Once Paul had asked to be sent to Rome, he was guarded by a Roman centurion day and night.

THE SHIPWRECK (*Contd.*)

After leaving Myra the winds had died down and it took them many days to reach Cnidus. From Cnidus they turned southwards, and passing Cape Salmone, on the eastern tip of Crete, eventually came to anchorage in the Fair Haven, a bay quite near to the city of Lasea.

Winter was now approaching and Paul advised the centurion to stay in the shelter of the bay, but the captain of the ship wanted to go on to Phenice, a larger bay on the south-west coast of the island. At first all went well and a gentle wind carried them in the right direction but then suddenly a fierce wind, known as Euroclydon, sprang up. Within a short while they were blown away from the coast of Crete and there was a danger they would run ashore on the island of Clauda. The only way to save the ship was to strike the sails and let the ship run before the storm. For many days the crew saw neither sun nor stars and they all felt they were certain to be drowned. The only cheerful voice was Paul's. He said, "Be of good cheer. No man shall lose his life. All that shall be lost is the ship. I have been told by an angel that I shall be brought before Cæsar and that all that sail with me shall be safe."

After fourteen days, at about midnight, the sailors thought they were coming near to land. Orders were given that soundings were to be taken. These showed the water was getting very shallow and it was decided to cast four stern anchors out and wait until daylight. The sailors began to be afraid and while they pretended to be lowering an anchor at the bow of the ship they were, in fact, trying to launch a boat to escape on their own. When Paul saw what they were doing he warned the centurion and the soldiers that without the help of the sailors they would all be doomed. The soldiers quickly took action and, cutting the ropes, let the boat drift away.

While they waited for daylight Paul suggested that they should all eat. This they did and were soon much more cheerful and hopeful of the outcome at daybreak.

When daylight came they could see a small creek with a sandy shore. The ship's cargo of wheat was thrown overboard to make it lighter, the sail was raised and the ship was allowed to run straight towards the shore so that it could run aground. The soldiers were afraid that in the confusion some of the prisoners might escape, and they suggested to the centurion that they should be killed, but he gave orders that every man should try and save himself. On boards and broken pieces of ship every man made his way safely to land as Paul had prophesied.]

Acts xxvii

ROME
PUTEOLI
RHEGIUM
SYRACUSE
MALTA
(MELITA)
CRETE
LASEA
CLAUDIA FAIR HAVENS
SALMONE
CNIDUS
MYRA
LYCIA
CYPRUS
SIDON
CAESAREA

THE
JOURNEY TO
ROME

PAUL'S ROUTE

A ROMAN SHIP
This was the kind of boat in which Paul was taken to Rome.

UNDERGIRDING A SHIP
During a storm there was a danger that the planks of a ship might spring apart. Ropes were passed round the ship to hold it together.

EUROCLYDON
This name was given to a strong north-east wind that blows in spring.

MALTA AND THE ROAD TO ROME

And when they were escaped, they knew that the island was called Melita. And the barbarous people shewed us no little kindness: for they kindled a fire, and received us every one, because of the rain and because of the cold. And when Paul had gathered a bundle of sticks, and laid them on the fire, there came a viper out of the heat, and fastened on his hand. When the barbarians saw the venomous beast hang on his hand they said among themselves, No doubt this man is a murderer, whom, though he hath escaped the sea, yet vengeance suffereth not to live. And he shook off the beast into the fire and felt no harm. Howbeit they looked when he should have swollen, or fallen down dead suddenly: but after they had looked a great while, and saw no harm come to him, they changed their minds, and said that he was a god.

In the same quarters were possessions of the chief man of the island, Publius, who received us, and lodged us three days courteously. It came to pass that the father of Publius lay sick of a fever: to whom Paul entered in, and prayed, and laid his hands on him, and healed him. When this was done, others also came and were healed. When we departed they laded us with such things as were necessary.

And after three months we departed in a ship of Alexandria, which had wintered in the isle, whose sign was Castor and Pollux. Landing at Syracuse, we tarried there three days. From thence we fetched a compass, and came to Rhegium: and after one day the south wind blew, and we came the next day to Puteoli: where we found brethren and were desired to tarry with them seven days: and so we went toward Rome. When the brethren heard of us they came to meet us as far as Appii forum, and The three taverns: whom when Paul saw, he thanked God, and took courage.

Acts xxviii.1-15

190

THE DEATH OF PAUL

Christians were killed by torture, lions, burning, or crucifixion. Paul, as a Roman citizen, was spared these, and beheaded instead.

THE LIFE OF PAUL	
	A.D.
Crucifixion of Jesus	30
Conversion of Paul	?35
First Journey	46-48
Second Journey	51-53
Third Journey	54-58
The Arrest	58
In Prison at Cæsarea	58-60
In Rome	61
Death of Paul	68

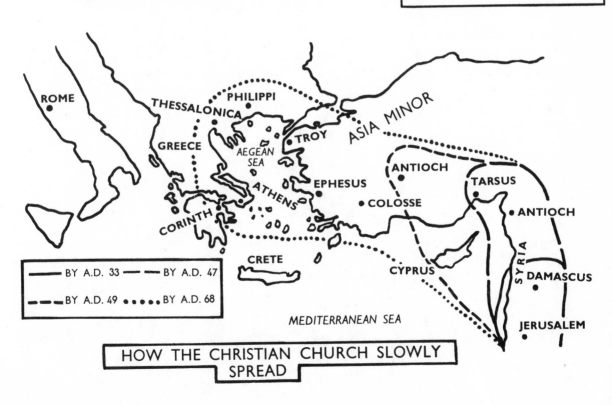

HOW THE CHRISTIAN CHURCH SLOWLY SPREAD